Buffalo Bill

Buffalo Bill

Scout, Showman, Visionary

FULCRUM
GOLDEN, COLORADO

Steve Friesen

Library of Congress Cataloging-in-Publication Data
Friesen, Steve, 1953-
  Buffalo Bill : scout, showman, visionary / by Steve Friesen.
      p. cm.
  Includes bibliographical references and index.
  ISBN 978-1-55591-719-7 (pbk.)
  1. Buffalo Bill, 1846-1917. 2. Pioneers--West (U.S.)--Biography. 3.
Entertainers--United States--Biography. 4. Wild west
shows--History--19th century. 5. West (U.S.)--Biography. I. Title.
  F594.B94F75 2010
  978'.02092--dc22
  [B]
                    2009044718

Printed in China
0 9 8 7 6 5 4 3 2 1

Design: Jack Lenzo
Cover image: Buffalo Bill Museum and Grave

Fulcrum Publishing, Inc.
4690 Table Mountain Drive, Suite 100
Golden, CO 80403
800-992-2908 • 303-277-1623
www.fulcrumbooks.com

Acknowledgments

This book is the result of fourteen years of living with Buffalo Bill. Nearly every day I walk past his clothing, saddles, guns, and *Wild West* posters as I go to my office in the Buffalo Bill Museum. As I took time to pull together my research, photograph the artifacts, and write this book, the museum staff that I am privileged to work with was not only very tolerant but helpful. I couldn't have done this book without the support of Betsy Martinson, Shelley Howe, Melanie Irvine, Angela Medbery, and David Samora. Collections consultant Peggy Schaller devoted many hours to the digitization project that enabled me to pull together information on the artifacts in the museum. A. J. Tripp-Addison, the superintendent of Denver Mountain Parks, was also very supportive and allowed me the time to work on it.

One of Buffalo Bill's greatest fans is Bill Carle. He grew up with Buffalo Bill, so to speak, after his family took over operation of the 1921 Pahaska Tepee when Johnnie Baker's widow died in 1957. The family continues to operate the gift shop in Pahaska Tepee under Bill's direction. Bill provided me with invaluable early photos of the museum, traveled with me on research trips, and has been a good friend.

Special mention needs to be made of the staff at the Buffalo Bill Historical Center (BBHC) in Cody, Wyoming, particularly those at the McCracken Library. Over the years, Paul Fees and Juti Winchester, both former curators at the BBHC, have provided useful information as well as stimulating conversations about Buffalo Bill.

My parents, Orlando and Barbara Friesen, first introduced me to Buffalo Bill by taking my family and me to historic sites and museums throughout the West. Evening discussions about all things historical with my wife, Monta Lee Dakin, also an historian of material culture, are a highlight of my day. Her support and advice have been invaluable for this book and for my career. Our children, Elizabeth and James, spent many hours at the Buffalo Bill Museum and endured many visits to historic sites while growing up. I'm pleased that, despite some complaining while they were teenagers, visits to museums and historic sites are now an important part of their adult lives.

My final acknowledgment is to William Frederick "Buffalo Bill" Cody. He truly was a visionary who made an indelible imprint on American culture.

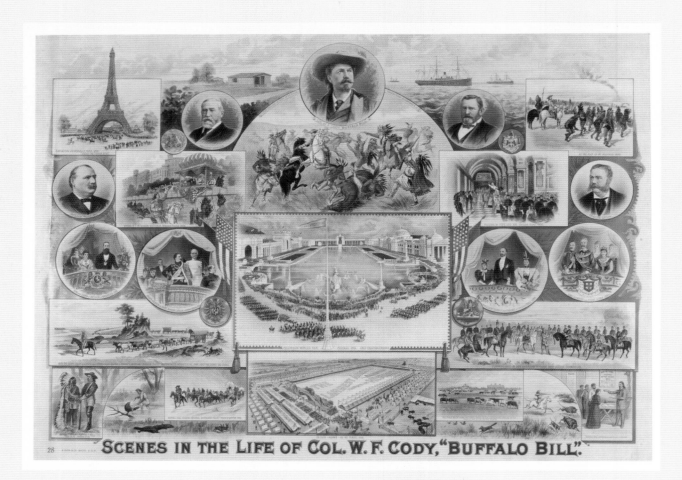

SCENES IN THE LIFE OF COL. W. F. CODY, "BUFFALO BILL".

Contents

Foreword

William F. "Buffalo Bill" Cody was America's first celebrity. He lived during a time of great geographic and technological expansion. It was also a time when American mass media became dominant. First it was the newspaper, present in every town and herald of civilization. Then, following the Civil War, dime novels and magazines like *Harper's Weekly* were nationally distributed. Coinciding with this was the perfection of the art of lithography, reproducing images in living color on posters and in publications. And finally, photographs and moving pictures enabled the wholesale and seemingly precise depiction of events. William F. Cody was there at every step, the right person in the right place at the right time. He had the flair, the charisma, and the savvy to attract the attention of the media and took advantage of each new technology. It was within this broadcast-communication factory that William F. Cody the man became Buffalo Bill the celebrity, and eventually Buffalo Bill the legend.

Long before Buffalo Bill's time, objects associated with saints and other legendary individuals were revered as relics and displayed in treasuries at cathedrals throughout Europe. The devout would undertake pilgrimages to see these treasures. Today, artifacts associated with legendary or famous persons are treated much the same. In America, people travel to George Washington's Mount Vernon, Elvis Presley's Graceland, and Henry Ford's Greenfield Village to see relics from these and other famous persons. Similarly, Denver's Buffalo Bill Museum and Grave on Lookout Mountain offers relics from William F. Cody and his contemporaries.

It was a treasury of sorts that a man named Johnny Baker envisioned when he proposed to open a museum on Lookout Mountain in 1920. Buffalo Bill Cody had been buried on the site less than three years earlier. Baker wrote to a representative of the City of Denver that as Cody's foster son and a performer in *Buffalo Bill's Wild West*, he had accumulated many mementos:

> At his death I become [*sic*] possessed of much of his personal effects such as his silver mounted saddles, bridles, guns, his buckskins he appeared in before the public. I have the hat he wore at his last public performance, Nov. 11th 1916, also the last cartridge he fired from a gun, a lock of his hair and the receipt for the last money he earned with his show. In fact I have a collection that would be of great interest to the visitors to Lookout Mountain, and if it is possible to get a location adjacent to his tomb, I would erect a building

to conform to the Architecture of the Mountain Parks scheme in which to display this collection.

Baker was granted permission to erect a building near Buffalo Bill's gravesite. It would house a museum, gift shop, and café. The new building, named Pahaska Tepee after Cody's hunting lodge near Yellowstone, opened to the public in May of 1921. The Buffalo Bill Memorial Museum, located within the building, was filled with relics that Baker had accumulated during his thirty-four years as protégé, friend, and foster son to Buffalo Bill. Some artifacts had come from Louisa, Cody's widow, and other family members. Other artifacts had been gifts to Buffalo Bill or Baker from performers, such as Sitting Bull and Short Bull, in *Buffalo Bill's Wild West*. During the ensuing years, the collection grew as first the Bakers and then a series of curators sought to collect and tell the man's complete story. It was the first museum dedicated to the life and times of Buffalo Bill.

There have been many biographies written about William F. "Buffalo Bill" Cody examining him as a historical or cultural figure. Based upon the collection of the Buffalo Bill Museum and Grave, descendant of Baker's Buffalo Bill Memorial Museum, this book aims to provide a new perspective on Cody by looking at his life as illuminated by the relics and artifacts left behind in his legendary wake.

Chapter One

A Life in the Outdoors

1846–1866

My love of hunting and scouting, and life on the plains generally, was the result of my early surroundings. *Buffalo Bill, 1879*

Surrounded by mementos of his life, Buffalo Bill relaxes in the parlor at his TE Ranch near Cody, Wyoming, circa 1912.

The photographer was ready. Buffalo Bill relaxed and leaned back slightly in his chair, holding his book as though he were deep in thought—the great scout in repose at his ranch. It was the sort of thing that his publicist, John Burke, was best at composing, a publicity piece for the masses. "The Great Scout in Repose." With luck it would drive more tourists to his properties outside Yellowstone National Park, all seeking to catch a glimpse of the great showman in an unguarded moment. Surrounded by the mementos of his life and facing one of his favorite paintings, it was easy to drop the show business persona and just be Will Cody.

In front of Cody was the painting *The Life I Love*, by C. S. Stobie. The painting depicted Cody with a hunting party in Wyoming, and it reminded him of happier, more carefree times. He had eaten with kings and queens, met with presidents, and rubbed elbows with the most famous people of his day. But he was never happier than when riding in the mountains and plains of the West.

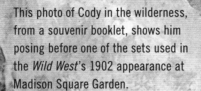

This photo of Cody in the wilderness, from a souvenir booklet, shows him posing before one of the sets used in the *Wild West*'s 1902 appearance at Madison Square Garden.

The wilderness within which Buffalo Bill grew up and that he loved was a common theme later in his *Wild West* shows. Posters for the *Wild West* showed both nature's beauty and fury. This is a romantic depiction of the wilderness from an 1893 poster printed by A. Hoen and Company.

Carefully crafted sets re-created western landscapes and enabled exciting reenactments of prairie fires, avalanches, and cyclones. A prairie fire was featured during the *Wild West*'s appearance in Madison Square Garden and was depicted in this 1886 poster.

Young Will escapes on Prince from proslavers, from Buffalo Bill's book *Story of the Wild West and Campfire Chats*, 1888.

William F. Cody was a child of the West. By the time he was twenty-one he had encountered nearly every adventure a young man could experience on America's frontier. Born in 1846 near Le Claire, Iowa, Cody moved with his family to a farm near Leavenworth, Kansas, when he was eight years old. There his father, Isaac, helped found the town of Grasshopper Falls, making several recruiting trips back East. It was at this early age that Cody developed his love of horses and riding, something that would stay with him and influence the development of his *Wild West* shows later in life. He later remarked that he "had been raised in the saddle" and "felt more at home there than in any other place." His first horse was Prince, a pony presented to him by his father.[1]

Young Will experienced several significant firsts near Leavenworth, Kansas. When the family arrived at Fort Leavenworth, he was initially impressed by the beauty of the surrounding scenery but became even more enthralled by the "vast number of white-covered wagons" camped in the valley. He pestered his father with many questions about the wagons and learned that they were poised to head west across the Great Plains. His sister Julia later wrote that Will was so excited that he declared that was what he wanted to do. Soon after, he met his first American Indians, members of the Kickapoo tribe, who came to trade with his father. They were very friendly, and young Cody endeavored to learn as much as he could about them. The peaceful nature of this first meeting and his fascination with the Indians gave him a positive attitude that would serve him well during his years as a scout and when he organized his *Wild West* shows.[2]

One day in 1854, Isaac was called to a public meeting in Leavenworth to speak upon the issue of slavery. When he spoke against Kansas becoming a slave state, a proslavery member of the crowd stabbed him. Will later wrote that his father shed "the first blood in the cause of the freedom of Kansas." His father recovered from the wound, but Isaac's life was later threatened several times and the family harassed for their anti-slavery stand. One day, eight-year-old Will was nearly captured as he rode Prince to warn his father that the pro-slavers were coming to kill him. The fleetness of Prince enabled him to out-distance them. The following year, pro-slavery forces once again visited the Cody home. Failing to find Isaac, they took Prince, and Will never saw him again.[3]

In 1857 Isaac became ill and, still in a weakened condition from the knife wound, died. At age eleven, Will Cody was now the man of the household. He wrote that "this sad event left my mother and the family in poor circumstances, and I determined to follow the plains for a livelihood for them and myself." While his father was still alive, Will had worked as a messenger and cattle herder for Russell, Majors and Waddell. The company was the largest of its kind in the West, sending wagon trains filled with freight to Santa Fe and other points west. After Isaac's death, the firm hired Will as a wagon driver, and he made the first of several trips across the Great Plains,

Eleven-year-old Will found early employment as a teamster on a wagon train transporting supplies across the plains.

This painting by C. S. Stobie hung in the parlor at Buffalo Bill's TE Ranch near Cody, Wyoming (see page 2). Stobie studied art before moving to Colorado in 1865. There he worked as a hunter and a scout, befriending Buffalo Bill, Wild Bill Hickok, Kit Carson, and other frontiersmen. The painting depicts a hunting trip Stobie took with Buffalo Bill in 1902.

This is one of several bowie-style knives owned by Cody. The size of the knife and the double edge near its tip made it useful both for hunting and as a weapon. The knife is well worn, suggesting years of use.

Buffalo Bill opened the Pahaska Tepee lodge just east of Yellowstone National Park in 1905. He gave the lodge his Lakota nickname, which meant "long hair." It acted as a wilderness refuge for Cody and his friends, as well as provided accommodations for park visitors. He wrote, "We go up there to eat, play cards, relax and rest for three or four weeks, and it brings back my old self."

This .30-caliber Winchester 1894 carbine was one of Cody's favorite hunting guns, given to him by Johnny Baker. He used it to shoot through this silver dollar.

from Leavenworth to Salt Lake City. These early trips had a marked impression upon young Cody, who marveled at the thrilling stories he heard from the other teamsters in the outfit. He observed that "the country was alive with buffaloes" and participated in his first buffalo hunt during the summer of 1857.[4]

Cody wrote in his autobiography that he met Wild Bill Hickok in 1857, when Hickok intervened to stop another teamster from bullying Will. "From that time forward Wild Bill was my protector and intimate friend, and the friendship thus begun continued until his death." While this specific encounter is questioned by some historians, Cody did indeed forge a lasting friendship with Hickok during this period of his life.[5]

Over the next several years, Will tried his hand at trapping, gold prospecting in Colorado during the 1859 gold rush, and even spent some time attending school in Leavenworth. But things like school held little fascination for him; it was the great expanse of the West that enthralled him. He wrote, "I longed for the cool air of the mountains; and to the mountains I determined to go."[6]

Will found his mountains by seeking employment with the Pony Express. Most of what is known about William Cody's teenage years comes from his autobiographies, biographies written by his sisters Julia and Helen, and a few accounts by boyhood friends. Some historians feel that these sources contain exaggerated and even fictional stories about Cody's life. Stories about Cody's employment with the Pony Express in particular have come under fire because of contradictory information about dates and activities. But Cody was indeed a frequent employee of Russell, Majors and Waddell, the company that started the Pony Express. A preponderance of witnesses from the period, including Alexander Majors himself, also stated that Cody was part of the Pony Express. Given this, Cody probably participated in the Pony Express in some form, if not as a regular rider.[7]

Those who question Cody's involvement with the Pony Express have suggested he invented his association with it to add to his reputation. Perhaps, but one could ask, Did William F. Cody become famous because of the Pony Express or did the Pony Express become famous because of William F. Cody? The Pony Express was short-lived, lasting only a year and a half. Were it not for the re-creation of a Pony Express ride in *Buffalo Bill's Wild West* for nearly thirty years, it might have ended up as a minor footnote in American history.

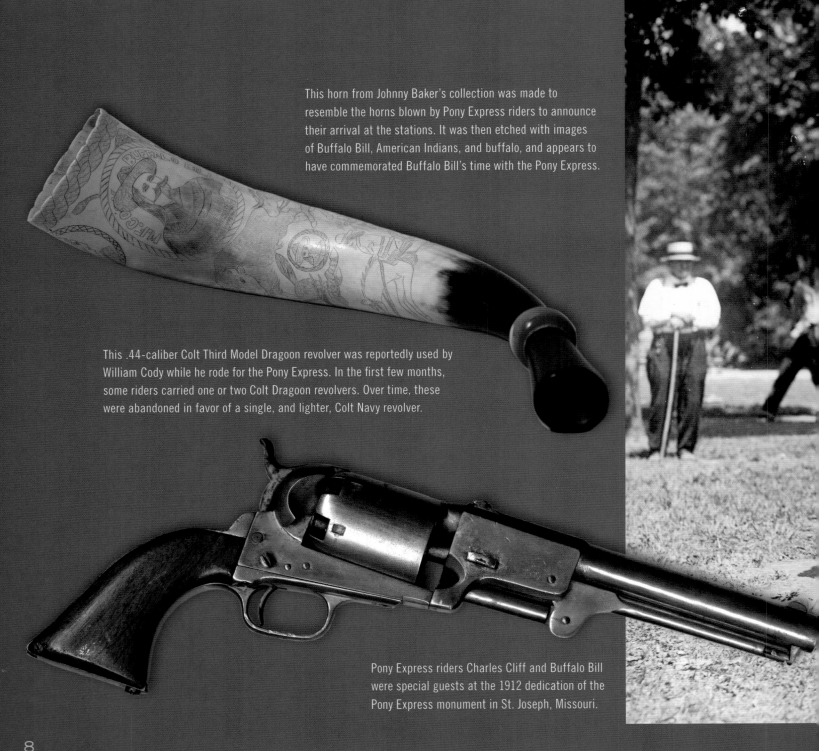

This horn from Johnny Baker's collection was made to resemble the horns blown by Pony Express riders to announce their arrival at the stations. It was then etched with images of Buffalo Bill, American Indians, and buffalo, and appears to have commemorated Buffalo Bill's time with the Pony Express.

This .44-caliber Colt Third Model Dragoon revolver was reportedly used by William Cody while he rode for the Pony Express. In the first few months, some riders carried one or two Colt Dragoon revolvers. Over time, these were abandoned in favor of a single, and lighter, Colt Navy revolver.

Pony Express riders Charles Cliff and Buffalo Bill were special guests at the 1912 dedication of the Pony Express monument in St. Joseph, Missouri.

THIS MONUMENT ERECTED BY THE
DAUGHTERS OF THE AMERICAN REVOLUTION
AND
THE CITY OF ST. JOSEPH
MARKS THE PLACE WHERE THE FIRST
PONY EXPRESS STARTED ON APRIL 3, 1860
1912

The conflict between proslavery and antislavery factions in Kansas broke into chaos with the beginning of the Civil War in 1861. Fifteen-year-old Will Cody, still angry about the attack that led to his father's death and the harassment of his family, joined a group of Jayhawkers, Kansas guerillas who preyed on their proslavery neighbors in Missouri. When his mother found out, she made him quit the group, saying they were little more than horse thieves. Later, most of his former companions were killed during a raid; Cody credited his mother with saving his life.[8]

Cody spent the summer of 1862 guiding military detachments across the Great Plains. When he returned to Kansas that fall, he was still interested in vengeance and soon joined another group of guerillas known as the Red Legs. The Red Legs claimed to support the Union cause but, like the Jayhawkers, attacked farms indiscriminately and seemed primarily interested in lining their own pockets. After less than a year, Cody returned to working with wagon trains, guiding and guarding them as they crossed the plains.[9]

In late 1863, Will's mother died. He became despondent and later wrote that after two months of carousing and "under the influence of bad whiskey, I awoke to find myself a soldier in the Seventh Kansas." Cody enlisted in the Seventh Kansas Volunteer Cavalry on February 19, 1864, and was mustered

Eighteen-year-old Will Cody at the time he enlisted in the Seventh Kansas Volunteer Cavalry.

out on September 29, 1865, after the Civil War ended.[10]

While Cody never served again as an enlisted man, the years of the Civil War were the beginning of a relationship between him and the army that continued until his death. He scouted and did other odd jobs on the Great Plains for around six months before moving to St. Louis to marry Louisa Frederici, whom he had met during the war. The couple moved to Leavenworth, and, for about six months, Cody tried to settle down. His efforts to run a hotel proved both financially unsuccessful and boring. Lured by the siren song of the great outdoors, he returned to what he knew best, roaming the Great Plains as a scout.

The stabbing of his father had a pro-found effect on young Will, who felt his father was an early martyr to the Union cause. He enlisted in the Seventh Kansas Volunteer Cavalry at age eighteen and, long after the Civil War, made gener-ous donations to veterans and veterans' causes. This commemorative cane was carved from a Rebel flagstaff that had been captured at the Battle of Shiloh and was presented to Cody by the Women's Relief Corps in 1883.

Buffalo Bill's father, stabbed by a proslaver, from Buffalo Bill's book *Story of the Wild West and Campfire Chats*, 1888.

Will Cody deeply cherished his mother and was devastated when she died. He often spoke and wrote of her. In this 1910 letter to Frank Winch he wrote, "I grew up among some of the roughest men and some of the most desperate characters that ever infested the border of civilization. And had it not been for [the] teaching and prayers of my mother I might have died with my boots on." He went on to say, "I think to our mothers we owe much. God bless our mothers."

Chapter Two
Will Cody Becomes Buffalo Bill

1867–1872

I immediately began my career as a buffalo hunter for the Kansas Pacific Railroad and it was not long before I acquired considerable notoriety. *Buffalo Bill, 1879*

Cody's reputation as a hunter later made his demonstrations of buffalo hunting a popular part of *Buffalo Bill's Wild West*.

The small group of buffalo gazed at the ground, searching for green shoots of grass. Buffalo Bill estimated that he could be on them in seconds. Beneath him he could feel Isham tensing his muscles. Isham was almost as good at hunting buffalo as Brigham had been. Cody raised his Winchester 1873 and gave the horse a gentle nudge with his knee. With a burst of speed, the pair, moving as one, was upon the small herd of buffalo. Coming up behind one of the bulls, Cody fired behind its shoulder and at its heart. It fell to its knees.

The crowd roared. They had just seen the great Buffalo Bill shoot a buffalo. But Cody was not pleased. He could not afford to lose one of the buffalo, that's why he used specially prepared blanks in his rifle. He wheeled Isham around and rode back to the bull. Thankfully, it had only been startled and was starting to get back up on its feet. If the bull had died, it could have been a problem. Back when Buffalo Bill got his nickname, there were millions

This .44-caliber Winchester Model 1873 rifle, with an octagonal barrel and a special chamber, was acquired by Buffalo Bill in 1907. It was probably used by Buffalo Bill for firing blanks while "hunting" buffalo during the *Wild West* show.

Buffalo Bill hunting buffalo while riding Brigham, from Buffalo Bill's *Story of the Wild West and Campfire Chats*, 1888.

of the large, hairy beasts; now the small herds at his ranch in Nebraska and in his show were among the few buffalo left.

During his first twenty years of life, Cody acquired a love for and knowledge of the West that would stay with him throughout his life. But it was the comparatively short six-year span from 1867 to 1872 that gave him both the nickname and the reputation upon which he built a lifelong career.

Will Cody hadn't planned on being a buffalo hunter. Isaac Cody had been part of a successful effort to found the town of Grasshopper Falls between 1855 and his death in 1857. Ten years later, Isaac Cody's son decided to follow in his footsteps and be a town founder. The railroad

was being built through Kansas, and Will Cody joined a partner in founding the town of Rome along its projected route. Unlike the first Rome, this community was built in nearly a day and, according to Cody, dissipated in just three days when a more competitive town was built a mile east of them. In reality, Rome did last longer than that, but it eventually disappeared because of competition from Hays, which today is one of the largest cities on Kansas's western plains.

His effort at town founding being as unsuccessful as his earlier effort at being a hotelier, Cody found employment providing meat for the Kansas Pacific Railroad. Assisted by his faithful horse Brigham, he proved to be quite an effective buffalo hunter. Cody wrote that "as soon as one buffalo would fall, Brigham would take me so close to the next, that I could almost touch it with my gun." His favorite hunting rifle was an 1866 Springfield, which he nicknamed Lucretia Borgia after the most famous member of the Borgias, an Italian Renaissance family known for its ruthless and deadly pursuit of power. The combination of Cody, Brigham, and Lucretia was similarly deadly when it came to buffalo hunting.[1]

Will Cody's prowess as a buffalo hunter spread, and it wasn't long before railroad workers started calling him Buffalo Bill. He was not, however, the only Bill who was an accomplished buffalo hunter. There was one other serious contender: Bill Comstock. While no newspaper accounts have been found that document a match between Cody and Comstock, there is both anecdotal and archaeological evidence that such a hunt was held. They met near the present-day town of Oakley, Kansas, and, accompanied by referees, proceeded to see who could kill the most buffalo in one day. By late afternoon, Cody had killed sixty-nine while Comstock had killed only forty-six. Cody was declared "champion buffalo hunter of the Plains" and his nickname of Buffalo Bill stuck.[2]

Over the course of seventeen months supplying meat to the railroad, Buffalo Bill killed 4,280 buffalo. When the railroad was completed, his buffalo-hunting services were no longer needed. From that time on, he confined his buffalo hunting to leading private hunting parties and occasionally providing buffalo meat to the army as part of his scouting services. During his entire lifetime, Cody probably killed fewer than 10,000 buffalo. That is a very small number when compared to the millions of buffalo that were alive in the years during which he hunted. The near extinction of the buffalo happened after Buffalo Bill's active hunting years.[3]

The years following his employment as a meat hunter were times of feast and famine for Buffalo Bill Cody. To save money, he sold Brigham and used horses supplied by the army while he was scouting. The demand for his services as a scout was sporadic, and the pay was not

This painting was presented to Buffalo Bill by E. W. Lenders on January 28, 1912. Cody considered Lenders "the best painter of buffaloes in the world." A German immigrant, Lenders divided his time between a studio in Philadelphia and trips to the West.

always very good. But when he did work, he performed well and significantly, ranging across western Kansas and Nebraska. He worked for generals Eugene A. Carr and Philip H. Sheridan, who praised his abilities. While Buffalo Bill wasn't becoming rich, he was certainly being noticed.

The Indian Wars began with the arrival of the first European settlers in the seventeenth century and continued through the end of the nineteenth century. The Indian Wars were a collection of skirmishes, conflicts, and all-out battles that frequently corresponded with westward migration. Buffalo Bill's military career during the latter 1860s and early 1870s coincided with the final bloody years of the Indian Wars. As a civilian scout, not a soldier, he worked under contract with the army. He was busiest in this capacity from 1868 to 1869, when he took part in nine battles.[4]

Johnny Baker commissioned this painting to be created by Denver artist Jakob Gogolin for placement in the Buffalo Bill Museum.

An efficient buffalo-hunting machine: Buffalo Bill, his horse Brigham, and a Springfield rifle.

This .50-caliber Model 1866 Springfield (Allin Conversion) could be the twin sister to Lucretia Borgia, Buffalo Bill's best-known buffalo-hunting rifle. According to Johnny Baker, Cody also used this rifle during his buffalo-hunting days.

17

Buffalo Bill killed his last buffalo in 1884. In 1915, he presented the mounted head to a fellow member of the Huckleberry Indians. The Huckleberry Indians were prominent businessmen who created the fraternity as part of the New York Athletic Club. Buffalo Bill was an honorary member.

Mr. Rudolph J. Schaefer,
114 East 51st Street,
New York City.

My dear "Chief":-

This is to certify that the Buffalo head which is in your possession is one which was taken from the carcass of the last Buffalo ever killed by me, and that one was shot on ...1884..... It seems good to know that it has fallen into the hands of an "Indian Chief" so well known to and so much esteemed by both the red man and the white man.

Sincerely,

W. F. Cody
"Buffalo Bill"

May 15, 1915.

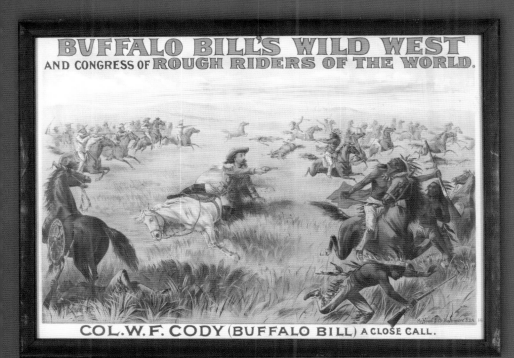

BUFFALO BILL'S WILD WEST
AND CONGRESS OF **ROUGH RIDERS OF THE WORLD.**

COL. W. F. CODY (BUFFALO BILL) A CLOSE CALL.

When Johnny Baker opened his museum near Cody's grave in 1921, he created an exhibit entitled Found on Indian Battlefields. The weapons in the exhibit were collected by Baker. They represented the Indian Wars and Buffalo Bill's early career in the wars.

This is an artillery saber (below) made by the Ames Manufacturing Company of Cabotville, Massachusetts. Ames produced most of the swords used during the Civil War. These in turn would have been used by members of the army when they moved West for the Indian Wars.

Issued by the Springfield Armory, this was originally a military weapon and was later sawed off at both ends to make a pistol. This alteration, plus the holes in the stock that were left by tacks, suggests that this particular weapon was used by an American Indian.

This .52-caliber Spencer Model 1863 rifle was a United States government-issue gun. Indians often decorated rifles with brass tacks; the tacks on this rifle suggest that an Indian used this gun.

This is one of 14,495 carbines made in Baltimore in 1861. It was purchased for cavalry use by the Union during the Civil War and then taken west after the war.

One of the most significant battles took Cody to Summit Springs, located in northeastern Colorado. A group of Cheyenne Dog Soldiers, led by Tall Bull, had been attacking white settlements in Nebraska and Kansas in 1868 and 1869. The Dog Soldiers were a warrior class known for their aggressiveness. Tall Bull's attacks had resulted in the deaths of many settlers and led to the capture of two white women. Guided by Will Cody, Frank North, and Luther North, the Fifth Cavalry was to rescue the women and put a stop to the Dog Soldiers' attacks. On July 11, 1869, Cody and the North brothers led a command of 244 soldiers and 50 Pawnee scouts to Tall Bull's village near Summit Springs. The command attacked the village, estimated to contain up to 500 inhabitants, killing more than 50 warriors and experiencing no casualties. They rescued one of the captives, but the other was killed just as the battle began. Cody was credited by General Eugene A. Carr, leader of the command, with killing Tall Bull.[5]

Although the Battle of Summit Springs was a major blow to the Dog Soldiers, the Indian Wars on the Great Plains had not yet ended. Over the next three years, Cody found himself in several actions, one of which earned him the Congressional Medal of Honor. Even though the engagement was not nearly as dramatic as the Battle of Summit Springs, his commanding officer felt he had acted in a valorous manner and recommended him for the honor. Years later, just one month after Cody's death in 1917, his Medal of Honor was rescinded because he had been a civilian scout at the time he received it. Seventy-two years after that, on January 12, 1989, the Medal of Honor was reinstated. The justification for the reinstatement concluded that the difference between his contract as a scout and enlistment as a soldier was not enough to negate the actions for which he received the medal in the first place.[6]

It was during this time of his life that Cody had a fateful meeting with Ned Buntline, the famed dime novelist. Buntline was seeking a colorful and charismatic figure for his next story, and Cody fit the bill. On July 24, 1869, Buntline joined Cody on a scouting trip from Fort McPherson, Nebraska, seeking a group of Indians that had attacked Union Pacific Railroad employees. They never caught up with the Indians, but Buntline pumped Cody with questions throughout the trip. The following December, Buntline combined Cody's answers and his own imagination to create "Buffalo Bill: The King of the Border Men," a serial story in the *New York Weekly*. It was the first of many stories that featured Cody.[7]

Cody's reputation began to spread as newspapers published accounts of his real exploits and dime novels created imaginary stories about him. By this time, Cody had settled down in

Buffalo Bill leads the cavalry into Tall Bull's village at Summit Springs, from Buffalo Bill's *Story of the Wild West and Campfire Chats*, 1888.

The engagement for which Buffalo Bill received the Congressional Medal of Honor (below) occurred on April 26, 1872. Buffalo Bill was awarded the Medal of Honor on May 22, 1872. Cody's Medal of Honor was in the possession of the Cody family at the time of his death and was given to the Buffalo Bill Museum on Lookout Mountain in 1921.

This medal (above) was presented to Buffalo Bill in 1890 by the Society of Veterans of Indian Wars.

BUFFALO BILL'S WILD WEST
AND CONGRESS OF ROUGH RIDERS
OF THE WORLD·

BUFFALO BILL TO THE RESCUE.

Buffalo Bill considered the Battle of Summit Springs one of the more important engagements of his scouting career. His role as rescuer in the battle was recounted in his various autobiographies, in printed *Wild West* programs, and in highly dramatic form on posters advertising his show.

Fort McPherson. Louisa had joined him in special quarters at the fort, bringing along their first child, Arta, and giving birth to their son, Kit Carson Cody. Fort McPherson was a staging point not only for scouting parties but also for buffalo hunts arranged for visiting dignitaries. As the best buffalo hunter in the area, Buffalo Bill was soon guiding visiting military officers such as General Philip H. Sheridan and foreign dignitaries such as the Earl of Dunraven around the Great Plains. During this time he also met Professor Othniel C. Marsh, a famous fossil hunter from Yale. Marsh was not seeking live buffalo, he was after the bones of ancient buffalo and other creatures that had wandered the Great Plains tens of thousands of years before.

Months earlier he had learned that Cody and some Pawnee scouts discovered bones that the Pawnees thought came from an ancient race of giants. Cody was fascinated with Marsh's stories about the dinosaurs and forged a lifetime friendship with the fossil hunter.[8]

Buffalo Bill was thrust into the limelight by one hunt in particular. The Grand Duke Alexis, in line for the throne of Russia, visited America with great pomp and circumstance in the winter of 1872. He had announced that he wished to kill a buffalo, so in preparation for the Grand Duke's visit, Cody found a suitable place for a hunting camp. He also engaged Lakota chief Spotted Tail and his warriors to join them at the camp. Spotted Tail's men were to demonstrate their method for hunting buffalo and entertain the Grand Duke and his entourage with a war dance. The Grand Duke arrived and the hunt began, with Alexis riding Cody's army-issue horse, Buckskin Joe. On his first several tries using a revolver, Alexis was unsuccessful. Finally, Cody loaned Alexis his rifle, Lucretia Borgia. With this assistance, the Grand Duke killed his first buffalo almost immediately, and the champagne corks were soon popping in his honor. The hunt continued for several days until Alexis moved on to his next destination. Reporters following the Grand Duke were fascinated by Buffalo Bill, who figured prominently in articles about the hunt.[9]

The Grand Duke Alexis kills his first buffalo while Buffalo Bill looks on, from Buffalo Bill's *Story of the Wild West and Campfire Chats*, 1888.

Buffalo Bill is the toast of Chicago society, from Buffalo Bill's *Story of the Wild West and Campfire Chats*, 1888.

After the hunt with the Grand Duke concluded, Cody received a leave of absence from his scouting duties to visit New York. Several gentlemen whom Cody had guided on a buffalo hunt during the previous year had invited him there. In many ways, the trip anticipated his future. As he moved his way eastward by rail, he made several stops. Accompanied by General Sheridan, he was the toast of Chicago society and was regaled with questions about life in the West. He would later visit Chicago many times, including a six-month stand during the 1893 World's Columbian Exposition. Accompanied by Professor Henry Ward, for whom he had supplied specimens for a natural history museum, Cody also toured the city of Rochester, New York, and dined with the mayor. This visit must have made a strong impression on Buffalo Bill, for he moved there a year later, in 1873. He made Rochester his home for nearly five years.[10]

Cody's trip to the East culminated in New York City, where he became part of the social whirl, dining at private clubs and attending social events, usually clad in buckskin. While Buffalo Bill was a stranger to New York, he was not unknown there. Buntline's serialized story about him had been published in the *New York Weekly* two years earlier, and news of his exploits, including the hunt with Duke Alexis, had been published in other local papers. He wrote, "I received numerous dinner invitations, as well as invitations to visit different places of amusement and interest; but as they came in so thick and fast, I soon became badly demoralized and confused." In the flurry, Buffalo Bill missed at least one important dinner engagement. But New York society's curiosity about this notorious western character overcame any sense of offense, and the invitations continued to arrive.[11]

Then, on February 20, 1872, Cody attended a very different sort of social engagement, an encounter that helped set the course for the rest of his life. Ned Buntline's story "Buffalo Bill: The King of the Border Men" had been turned into a play and was to open at the Bowery Theatre. Cody wrote, "I was curious to see how I would look when represented by someone else, and of course I was present on opening night, a private box having been reserved for me." He was invited onstage between acts and was introduced to the audience. Faced not by thousands of buffalo or hundreds of Indians but simply confronted by a sea of faces, Cody was nearly speechless. Later that evening, the manager of the play offered him a salary of $500 a week to join the play as himself. Cody declined, but the idea was planted. A year later, he would be an actor.[12]

The 1872 visit of Russian Grand Duke Alexis for a buffalo hunt in the West added to Buffalo Bill's fame. After the Duke failed to kill a buffalo with his pistol (shown above in *Frank Leslie's Illustrated Newspaper*), Cody loaned him Lucretia Borgia. Using Cody's rifle the Duke felled a buffalo immediately. Within three years Lucretia Borgia was no longer useable, her stock broken when Buffalo Bill fended off the charge of an elk.

SPECIAL TIME CARD
FOR THE TRAIN CONVEYING
His Imperial Highness
THE
Grand Duke Alexis
OF RUSSIA
OVER THE
ST. LOUIS KANSAS CITY & NORTHERN RAILWAY
FROM
ST. LOUIS TO KANSAS CITY.
THURSDAY JANUARY 11, 1872.
W. H. ARTHUR Gen'l Sup't.   T. B. BLACKSTONE President.

Chapter Three
Buffalo Bill's New Career

1873–1878

My new drama was arranged for the stage by J. V. Arlington, the actor. It was a five-act play, without head or tail, and it made no difference at which act we commenced the performance.
Buffalo Bill, 1879

J. Knox O'Neil, a contemporary of Buffalo Bill, painted this portrait of him as a successful eastern businessman with western accessories of long hair and hat.

It was almost curtain time, and Buffalo Bill had a few moments to think. Before he left the show, Wild Bill Hickok had said they were fools. Pity that grown men had to run around onstage making laughingstocks of themselves; there had to be a more respectable way to make a living. But the theater paid much better than scouting, and there was always the break in the theatrical season during the summer. Then he could revisit the plains, hunt, and refresh himself before returning to the stage. That visit to New York several years earlier had certainly changed his life.

Cody had prolonged his New York trip during the spring of 1872, staying in the city for several weeks before General Sheridan called him back to his scouting duties in the West. After Cody returned to Nebraska, Ned Buntline, who had seen how the New York audience reacted to Buffalo Bill onstage, pestered him throughout the summer and fall with a series of letters. Buntline thought that, with Buffalo Bill as a headliner, there was good money to be made on the theater circuit.

Lured by the comparatively lucrative salary offered by acting and deciding he didn't have much to lose, Bill Cody resigned his scouting contract barely eight months after returning to the Great Plains. After all, who better to play Buffalo Bill than himself, and,

Buffalo Bill with fellow actors Ned Buntline and Texas Jack Omohundro. Buffalo Bill and Texas Jack are both wearing buffalo-hide coats from their hunting and scouting days. Buffalo Bill frequently wore beaded moccasins onstage, a practice he gave up once he began *Buffalo Bill's Wild West*.

as Cody put it, it was time to "try my luck behind the footlights." Cody was accompanied in this endeavor by his friend Texas Jack Omohundro. Texas Jack and Cody had scouted together for several years. Omohundro had been one of the less visible participants in several buffalo hunts with Cody, plus the hunt with Grand Duke Alexis. Like Buffalo Bill, his exploits as a scout had been mentioned in newspaper articles and he had a growing reputation back East. On December 12, 1872, the two scouts met Ned Buntline in Chicago, where they were to stage their first play.[1]

Buntline immediately began advertising *Scouts of the Prairie*, an as-yet-unwritten play that would open on December 16. It would star Buffalo Bill and Texas Jack playing themselves, while Buntline would write a role for himself. Buntline dashed off a script in four hours, and the two scouts began the task of memorizing their lines. In the meantime, Buntline gathered a supporting cast that included the noted Italian ballerina Mademoiselle Giuseppina Morlacchi. The playbill was thus built on four fairly well-known personalities of the time. Morlacchi had introduced the cancan to America, Buntline was well-known as a dime novelist, and Cody and Omohundro had some notoriety as scouts. Morlacchi and Buntline had a little acting experience, but Buffalo Bill and Texas Jack had none at all.[2]

The combination of Buffalo Bill, Texas Jack Omohundro, Ned Buntline, and Mademoiselle Morlacchi proved popular. After such a successful season, Buffalo Bill and Texas Jack were disappointed to discover their income was not much more than they would have received had they continued scouting. Sure that they could do better, they broke away from Buntline and started their own show.

One of the oldest remaining letters from Buffalo Bill, this note was written to a fan, James Russell, in 1873. It thanks him for a keg of whiskey that he sent to Cody and Texas Jack and invites him to join them on a hunt out West.

HON. WILLIAM F. CODY.

Wild Bill Hickok joined his friends Buffalo Bill and Texas Jack for part of their 1873–74 season, then left the show and returned to the West. Texas Jack left the show after 1876, leaving Buffalo Bill as its primary celebrity. The Nathaniel Orr Company, which provided the engraving of Buffalo Bill used on this Combination poster, also supplied the engravings for Cody's dime novels.

Acting experience ended up being of little importance to the audience that flocked to the *Scouts of the Prairie* debut. They were there to see the two persons they had read about in the papers: Buffalo Bill and Texas Jack. The show was a success, despite one critic's characterization of Cody as "a good-looking fellow, tall and straight as an arrow, but ridiculous as an actor." Other critics noted Cody's manner of charming the audience and the realism he brought to his performance. Actor or not, Buffalo Bill was a showman.[3]

Following a week in Chicago, the play moved on to St. Louis. There, Cody was briefly reunited with his wife, Louisa. When Bill quit his army contract and left Fort McPherson for Chicago, she had taken the children to live with her family in St. Louis. By this time Louisa was caring for Arta, Kit, and a new child, Orra. Shortly after the appearance in St. Louis, Cody moved his family, first to live near relatives in West Chester, Pennsylvania, then to Rochester, New York, where he purchased a home. This must have been an attempt to keep them closer as he moved into a new career that was clearly more focused on the East than the West. Separations due to Will's work had been common during the couple's seven years of marriage. Despite his effort to keep his family close by, with his entry into show business, these separations were to grow more frequent in occurrence and duration. The show moved back East, playing a variety of small towns and cities that included Cincinnati, Boston, and Philadelphia, then finally closing in New York after six months.[4]

During Buffalo Bill's first appearance onstage, he completely forgot his lines. With prompting from Ned Buntline, he improvised through the entire play. From that date on, he rarely followed the scripts that he was provided.

Cody's move East to become an actor introduced him to a whole new style of clothing. Onstage he wore the garb of a frontiersman, but as a resident of Rochester, New York, and a budding celebrity, he needed to be more formal. He grew to be as comfortable in fancy dress as in buckskins—always, of course, wearing a Stetson hat.

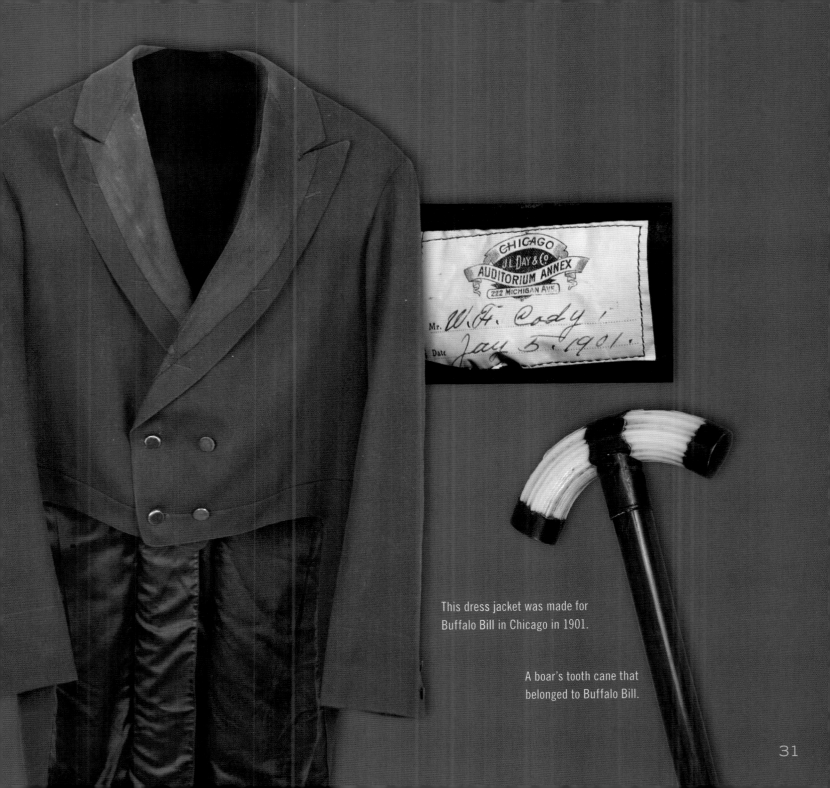

This dress jacket was made for Buffalo Bill in Chicago in 1901.

A boar's tooth cane that belonged to Buffalo Bill.

31

In June, at the conclusion of their very successful first season, Cody and Omohundro were disappointed to find their profits were less than $250 per week. Buntline had pocketed the lion's share of the show's income. The two scouts returned to Nebraska for several weeks of hunting and discussions about their future onstage. Reinvigorated by their respite on the plains, they returned to New York and set about organizing their own acting company.[5]

When the acting company premiered *Scouts of the Plains* that fall, it included a new player who was as well-known as Buffalo Bill and Texas Jack. Cody's old friend Wild Bill Hickok had joined the troupe. Mademoiselle Morlacchi, now married to Texas Jack, was once again part of the cast. Accompanying them as publicist, show manager, and occasional cast member was John M. Burke. Burke had been an actor, dramatic troupe manager, and newspaper editor, all skills that he employed in his role with the company. This was the beginning of a relationship between Burke and Buffalo Bill that would last until Cody's death. Burke had the discipline and marketing acumen to turn Buffalo Bill's flair and flamboyance into a marketable commodity. Where Cody was the consummate showman, Burke was the perfect publicist.

Scouts of the Plains was a hit, and soon Cody was earning the kind of money he had expected to make while working with Buntline. Wild Bill Hickok, however, did not prove to be as great of an asset to the show as Buffalo Bill had hoped. He wasn't very serious about the work and felt they were making fools of themselves. He drank heavily and got into fights with everyone from members of the audience to cast members. The situation came to a head when the acting company appeared at a theater in Rochester, Cody's new hometown. Hickok reneged on a promise to be on his best behavior, and the two argued. Even though they made up later, Hickok decided to leave the troupe. He had appeared with the company for six months. It was the last time Cody would see his old friend.[6]

In 1875, Buffalo Bill wrote his first dime novel. Over the following decade, a number of dime novels appeared with his name as author. While some, particularly the later ones, were probably the work of ghostwriters, many were written by Cody. The culmination of these writing efforts was the penning of his autobiography in 1879. Historians are divided as to the truth of many of the stories in the autobiography, but most agree that Cody's experience writing dime novels certainly had some influence upon the way he told his life story. The autobiography would be revised, republished, and even serialized many times before Cody's death in 1917.[7]

The United States' centennial was in 1876, and Buffalo Bill's new play, *Life on the Border*, did well as the nation

Buffalo Bill and Wild Bill Hickok were friends, scouts, buffalo hunters, and appeared onstage together. Because of these similarities, they have often been mistaken for each other. Artist Robert Lindneux, who knew Cody but not Hickok, painted portraits of them in 1933 that emphasized their similarities.

Hickok died at age thirty-nine after being shot in the back of the head in a Deadwood saloon; Cody died at age seventy, not many years after visiting his old friend's grave. As these locks of hair from Johnny Baker's collection show, Hickok's hair never had a chance to turn gray.

Lock of Buffalo Bill's Hair

Lock of Wild Bill's Hair

celebrated its past and future. Around this time, publicity for the acting company began to refer to it as the Buffalo Bill Combination. Texas Jack and Mademoiselle Morlacchi were managing their own careers but still appeared

BEADLE'S Dime New York Library

Copyrighted, 1878, by BEADLE AND ADAMS.

No. 52. Published Every Wednesday. *Beadle & Adams, Publishers,* 98 WILLIAM STREET, NEW YORK. Ten Cents a Copy. $5.00 a Year. Vol. IV.

Death Trailer, the Chief of Scouts;

Or, LIFE AND LOVE IN A FRONTIER FORT.

BY BUFFALO BILL---Hon. William F. Cody.

ONE MIGHTY LEAP, A BENDING OF THE RIDER'S BODY, AND THE GALLANT ANIMAL CAME DOWN SAFE WITHIN THE INCLOSURE.

Of the fifteen dime novels attributed to Buffalo Bill in the 1870s, *Death Trailer, the Chief of Scouts* was likely written by him. Published in 1878, it was the last dime novel attributed to Cody before the release of his autobiography in 1879.

occasionally in Buffalo Bill's plays. Their sporadic presence and the loss of Wild Bill Hickok as a headliner did not seem to affect attendance. It was becoming clear that the force of Buffalo Bill's name and personality was enough to draw crowds.

Cody turned thirty in February of 1876. Any joy he felt in passing that milestone was tempered by the death of his five-year-old son, Kit, on April 22. Cody was performing in Massachusetts when he got word that Kit was deathly ill with scarlet fever. He took an overnight train to Rochester and arrived in time to be with Kit during his last hours. Cody was devastated. But it was not the last death that would touch his life that year.[8]

For several years, gold hunters had been encroaching on Cheyenne and Lakota lands in the Black Hills of South Dakota. The resulting tension came to a head with open conflict in the summer of 1876. When he learned of this, Buffalo Bill decided to cut the 1876 theatrical season short, telling his audience that he was off to the Indian Wars. On June 10, he signed on as chief of scouts with the Fifth Cavalry. Several weeks later, on July 7, he was stunned to learn of the defeat of Custer at Little Bighorn on June 25. George Armstrong Custer and Buffalo Bill had met several times, with Cody providing scouting services to Custer on one occasion. The loss of Custer and his command was also a major blow to a nation preparing to celebrate its 100th anniversary on July 4.[9]

Best known as an illustrator, E. W. Deming spent over thirty years with different American Indian tribes making field sketches of their cultures. While this painting of warriors charging Custer and his men is historically inaccurate, it effectively captures the action of the Last Stand and the desperation of the soldiers under Custer's command.

Curley, a Crow scout, and Comanche, Captain Myles Keogh's horse, were the only members of Custer's command to survive the Battle of Little Bighorn. Curley escaped by blending in with the attacking Lakota and Cheyenne. In 1886, Curley joined *Buffalo Bill's Wild West*, and Johnny Baker later acquired his bow and arrows.

On July 17, Buffalo Bill led a party of troopers in an action against a group of Cheyenne warriors at Warbonnet Creek. Eyewitness Christian Madsen later recorded that Cody was ahead of the party and fired at Cheyenne subchief Yellow Hair, killing him. Yellow Hair received that name because of a trophy he wore, the scalp of a blond woman. According to Cody, after he killed Yellow Hair, he then removed his scalp, waving it in the air shouting, "The first scalp for Custer." He later sent Yellow Hair's scalp, warbonnet, and weapons back home to Rochester for display in the window of his friend Moses Kerngood's store. The story of the "first scalp for Custer" as well as the scalp itself became a central part of the publicity for the Buffalo Bill Combination troupe as well as for *Buffalo Bill's Wild West* later. Of the many stories about Buffalo Bill, this was perhaps most repeated during his lifetime and after his death.[10]

Like many stories, "The First Scalp for Custer" grew in the telling, with embellishments added by Cody and his various publicists. Over time it was ritualized into a duel that included challenges and taunts hurled by Yellow Hair and Buffalo Bill. The story was also portrayed many times on engravings, paintings, and even advertising posters. Despite the hyperbole, Madsen, probably the most reliable of the eyewitnesses, referred to the event upon which the story was based as an almost chance meeting.

Charles King, who was also present when Buffalo Bill took Yellow Hair's scalp, reported that Cody wore a flamboyant Mexican vaquero outfit to the fight. This account has been frequently repeated, often with the conclusion that Buffalo Bill dressed in a stage costume for the fight, knowing it would be useful to his show-business persona. There is no question that Cody later used the incident for publicity. The suggestion, however, that he was posturing for promotional purposes diminishes the seriousness of the event and is based upon what appears to be a questionable account.[11]

Christian Madsen disputed Charles King's account of the fight at Warbonnet Creek, saying it was more romance than fact. The idea that Cody put on a showy outfit for the battle, while it might be romantic, makes little sense. Of all the accounts about the first scalp for Custer, King's is the only one that suggests Cody wore something out of the ordinary for a scout. It is hard to imagine that he kept a special costume in reserve for just the right moment, particularly since the Fifth Cavalry would have been traveling light. It also assumes that he knew there would be a significant fight on that particular day out of the several weeks they had been on the trail and then took time to change for it. If Cody did put on a stage costume for promotional purposes, he never took advantage of it. His own promotional materials associated with the incident always showed him in scout's attire.

The only mention of it is in King's account, which is oft repeated by historians. No other publications of the period refer to Cody as wearing the stage costume.[12]

The story of the killing of Yellow Hair, like the earlier story of Summit Springs and the killing of Tall Bull, helped build a reputation for Cody as an Indian fighter. While this reputation was useful for launching and maintaining his show business career, it was much exaggerated. Cody killed very few American Indians during his years as a scout and always did so under combat situations. Even the taking of Yellow Hair's scalp, a practice that American Indians considered honorable and which many scouts copied, was a one-time act. Later in life he often remarked that he regretted the killing he had to do during the Indian Wars.

Buffalo Bill's "first scalp for Custer," taken on July 17, 1876, helped create his reputation as an Indian fighter. This illustration, from Cody's 1879 autobiography, *The Life of Hon. William F. Cody Known as Buffalo Bill the Famous, Hunter, Scout and Guide*, was the first visual depiction of the event.

After Buffalo Bill's death, some people questioned whether he had actually taken the "first scalp for Custer." In the 1920s, Johnny Baker began a project to authenticate the story and place a monument where Buffalo Bill killed Yellow Hair. He contacted Christian Madsen, Charles King, and other eyewitnesses to help locate the spot. A map was created by American Indians who had witnessed the fight, and Madsen added his notes (in red). Baker died before the monument was completed in 1934, but his widow, Olive, attended the dedication with Madsen.

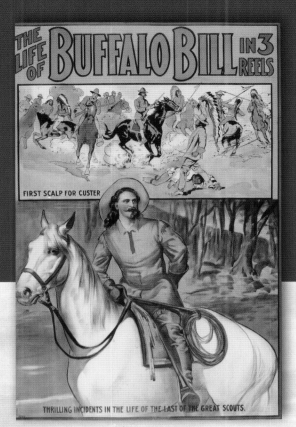

Buffalo Bill's "First Scalp for Custer" proved to be popular with audiences. It was featured in *Buffalo Bill's Life in Three Reels* and a documentary on the Indian Wars, movies produced by Cody near the end of his life. In this photograph, Buffalo Bill re-creates the scalping for his Indian Wars documentary.

Just two weeks after Cody killed Yellow Hair, his friend Wild Bill Hickok was shot in the back of the head in Deadwood, South Dakota. The date was August 2, 1876. Buffalo Bill later wrote, "Thus ended the career of a life-long friend of mine who, in spite of his many faults, was a noble man, ever brave and generous hearted." Cody continued scouting on the Great Plains until September, then returned to New York. The summer months of 1876 would be the last time he scouted for the army.[13]

That fall, the Buffalo Bill Combination opened a new season in Rochester. Building on Cody's reputation from the preceding summer, the Combination now offered a new play, *Red Right Hand; or, Buffalo Bill's First Scalp for Custer.* The season continued through June of 1877, with appearances in California, Kansas, Nebraska, and Nevada. While Cody had been warned that his entertainments about western life might not be well-received in the West, the Combination played to full houses. At the end of the season, he stopped in Denver to see his sisters, then joined his old scouting companion Frank North in Nebraska. There he and North had purchased land not far from North Platte, intending to use it for ranching. In the fall of 1877, the Combination resumed touring, and the next year the Cody family moved from Rochester to a new home in North Platte. After five years in the East, they established residency in the West for good.[14]

Buffalo Bill had taken a great risk by moving East in 1872. As he put it, "I was leaving a comfortable little home, where I was sure of making a good living for my family; while, on the other hand, I was embarking on a sea of uncertainty." He started a new career with which he had no experience and moved his family to a place unlike anywhere they had lived before. The risk, however, paid off. By the time he moved his family to North Platte in 1878, the Buffalo Bill Combination was a success, bringing in more money than he had imagined. That, however, was not enough for Will Cody.

Chapter Four
Seeking Authenticity

1879–1886

I conceived the idea of organizing a large company of Indians, cow-boys, Mexican vaqueros, famous riders and expert lasso throwers, with accessories of stage coach, emigrant wagons, bucking horses and a herd of buffaloes, with which to give a realistic entertainment of wild life on the plains. *Buffalo Bill, 1888*

THE BRONCHO BUSTERS BREAKING IN THEIR FRACTIOUS STEEDS.
AN ACT THAT IS NEVER TWICE ALIKE AND FULL OF DAREDEVIL FUN.

Buffalo Bill remarked that "only a most expert rider could be a cow-boy, as it requires the greatest dexterity and daring in the saddle to cut a wild steer out of the herd." "Cowboy Fun," which exhibited these skills of riding, was an important act in *Buffalo Bill's Wild West*.

After six weeks in the saddle rounding up cattle on his Nebraska ranch, Buffalo Bill was exhausted but excited. A lot of people made fun of cowboys, but they had no idea of the skill that the work required. These men demonstrated amazing horsemanship and were dead-on shots with a lasso. If only the folks who came to see his Combination could see cowboys working in a roundup and American Indians riding in full war paint, whooping it up while attacking a settler's wagon. Now that would be exciting. But there was barely enough room onstage for a gunfight, let alone cowboys and Indians riding horses. Cody wished the audience could see what life in the West was really like.[1]

By 1877, Buffalo Bill had realized that his plays could, and should, be more than simple melodramas. He knew that people did not come to see them for the stories; nobody seemed to care about the scripts. People came to see the Buffalo Bill Combination perform because they wanted a glimpse of what was going on in the West. They wanted to see scouts from the prairie and they wanted to see Buffalo Bill, the man who took the first scalp for Custer. What they wanted was a realistic, exciting depiction of life in the West.

Cody already had real frontier characters like Captain Jack Crawford in his troupe. If a realistic depiction was to be made, American Indians could no longer be played by white actors. Buffalo Bill needed real Indians. When his new show opened in the fall of 1877, it included two Lakota chiefs he had recruited that summer. Entitled *May Cody; or, Lost and Won*, the show revolved around a recent event on the frontier, the Mountain Meadows Massacre. While the entire piece was still greatly dramatized, Buffalo Bill was clearly moving in the direction of depicting actual life and adventures.[2]

With the addition of real Indians, the Buffalo Bill Combination continued to play to packed houses. Yet something was missing. After an 1879 appearance by the Combination at the Central City Opera House in Colorado, a critic from the local paper complained that the play had none of the bears and buffalo that one might expect in the West. Just before the Central City appearance, the Combination appeared in a Denver playhouse. It was remarked that live Lakota Indians and a burro were major attractions of the show. But except for the Indians, the other western characters, and the burro, there wasn't much

more. The wide-open expanse of the West with its variety of peoples and animals simply couldn't be conveyed on the small stage of a playhouse.[3]

The time had come to transcend the limitations of the stage. Cody wanted to re-create the West that he had experienced and that he saw was vanishing.

Prairie Waif, A Story of the Far West was first performed in 1880. In accordance with Cody's efforts to add authenticity to his plays, it included several Indian warriors. The final performance of *Prairie Waif*, marking the end of the Combination, was in Denver on April 10, 1886.

JOHNSON HALL

One Night,

Wednesday Feb. 28.

The most celebrated of all American Characters the original and famous Government Scout, Guide and Indian Fighter.

Buffalo Bill

HON. W. F. CODY.

In his Greatest Play, written by Chas. Foster, entitled

20 Or Buffalo Bill's **20**
DAYS —Pledge!— **DAYS**

25 —A Company of Superior Artists— 25
6 —Celebrated Winnebago Indian Chiefs— 6
A Sensational Daily Street

FREE— . Parade. —FREE
—A host of New—
STARTLING Specialties STARTLING
—New and Splendid—
ORIGINAL Scenic Effects. ORIGINAL

The Sensation of the Season!

PRICES AS USUAL. Reserved Seats now on sale
at Blanchard's. 1w3

From the *Kennebec Reporter*, Gardiner, Maine, February 24, 1883.

Buffalo Bill in Twenty Days; or, Buffalo Bill's Pledge was the last play written for the Buffalo Bill Combination. It was performed between 1882 and 1884. This is one of the few scripts still in existence from a Buffalo Bill Combination play.

He later wrote, "Such exhibitions as I had prepared to give could only be shown in large open-air enclosures." So he began what he described as a "Herculean undertaking," gathering the necessary animals, people, and props for a grand spectacle. This undertaking was the first of its kind and, even after it was copied by competitors, the most popular.[4]

On July 4, 1882, Buffalo Bill assisted the town of North Platte with its annual Fourth of July celebration. Building on his previous experience with roundups at his ranch, Cody added riding and roping contests to the celebration. While his experience in organizing the event undoubtedly influenced his later efforts to create what would become *Buffalo Bill's Wild West*, it was not, as some have asserted, the origin of the show. The celebration's only coverage was by the *Omaha Bee*, and then the event was not mentioned again. Cody himself did not even refer to it several years later when he wrote about the founding of the *Wild West* in his book *Story of the Wild West and Campfire Chats*. In fact, the occasion seems to have been given no importance at all until twenty years later, when promoter Louis E. Cooke began crediting it with being the progenitor of the *Wild West*, calling it the "Old Glory Blowout."

Cooke found willing corroboration for his tale on the part of the people of North Platte, who adjusted their memories accordingly. Soon their recollections of the Fourth of July included statements by Buffalo Bill that he was so pleased by the celebration that he would have to create a show just like it. One gentleman even remembered Cody saying that he would call it *Buffalo Bill's Wild West and Congress of Rough Riders*. The show did not, however, receive that title until after Nate Salsbury added the rough riders component in the 1890s. The following spring, Cody's new undertaking bore little resemblance to the 1882 celebration. Buffalo Bill's *Wild West* was not inspired by a single event but was built on his experiences in the West.[5]

Buffalo Bill drew upon his contacts throughout the West to make his idea a reality. His friend A. H. Patterson of Fort Collins, Colorado, provided wild elk and burros for a pack train. The buffalo and bears that had been missing from his stage show were acquired elsewhere in the West. Performers included cowboys and vaqueros, Pawnee and Lakota Indians, members of brass bands from western towns such as Fort Collins, and several well-known performers; in all a troupe totaling fifty-one people. Foremost among these were national champion sharpshooters Captain A. H. Bogardus and William F. "Doc" Carver. Carver, Bogardus, and Cody would all provide exhibitions of marksmanship during the program. Cody's fellow scout and rancher Frank North was another headliner. Thirteen years earlier, North, together with Cody, had gained some notoriety during the Battle at Summit

Young Johnny Baker learned marksmanship from his foster father, Buffalo Bill. He joined the *Wild West* cast in 1883 and was known as The Cowboy Kid.

Springs. Their mutual friend and Cody's earlier stage partner Texas Jack Omohundro would probably have joined the group had he not died of pneumonia in Leadville, Colorado, in 1880. Two other members of the first cast would become well-known over time: Buck Taylor, a big Texas cowboy, and John Y. Nelson, a mountain man and scout.[6]

The cast included two newcomers who would be associated with Cody until his death. One of them was a young man from Oklahoma who served as an interpreter for the Pawnee. Gordon Lillie, nicknamed Pawnee Bill, stayed with Buffalo Bill for two seasons before starting his own rival *Wild West* show. Twenty-five years later, he became a partner with Buffalo Bill. The other newcomer was thirteen-year-old Johnny Baker. Cody had met Baker in North Platte several years earlier. Baker, who idolized Buffalo Bill, was the same age that Cody's son, Kit, would have been had he not died of scarlet fever. Cody treated young Johnny like his own son, teaching him to shoot and nicknaming him The Cowboy Kid. Baker stayed with Buffalo Bill until Cody's death in 1917.[7]

Champion marksman William "Doc" Carver was Buffalo Bill's partner during the first year of operation. After some discussion, the name *The Wild West, Cody and Carver's Rocky Mountain and Prairie Exhibition* was chosen. John Burke, who had been publicist for the Buffalo Bill Combination, continued in that position for the new show. *Show* was, however, a term that he and Cody rejected. It was not a show at all; it was an educational exhibition. As such, the term *show* was never used in its title nor in any official materials. Burke would later emphasize this whenever he oriented new staff members. Members of the *Wild West* who used the word would be fired. It was an authentic portrayal of the West, not a common melodrama or medicine show.[8]

One of the most famous components of the exhibition was neither a person nor an animal. After the Civil War, during the winter of 1866, Cody spent several months as a stagecoach driver between Kearney and Plum Creek, Nebraska. Based on these and other experiences, he knew that a stagecoach wheeling at full speed around an arena would excite audiences. Sensing also that the stagecoach, despite its many discomforts, would evoke certain romantic and adventurous visions of the disappearing Old West, Cody incorporated an attack upon a stagecoach into his program. But he didn't use just any stagecoach. He used the Deadwood Stage. Deadwood, where his friend Wild Bill Hickok had been killed, fit the stereotype of the untamed western town perfectly. It evoked visions of unfettered violence, a frenzied gold rush, and was at the heart of the incursions that led to the Lakota and Cheyenne uprisings that resulted in Little Bighorn. He was right. The Deadwood Stage was a hit and became a central part of the *Wild West* for its entire thirty years of operation.[9]

Dress rehearsals for the *Wild West* were held at the fairgrounds in the town of Columbus, Nebraska, Frank North's hometown. Its grand opening was held on May 17, 1883, in Omaha, Nebraska. Newspaper accounts stated that ten thousand attended its first performance and twenty thousand attended its second performance that day. One account noted that the audience "cheered at trifles and blazed with enthusiasm at any demonstration of merit. The picture was an extraordinary one, such as we are not likely to see again."[10]

While the *Wild West* would indeed be seen again, for the next three decades, one of its founding members left the show after the first season. Doc Carver had adopted the nickname Evil Spirit of the Plains. The persona fit him all too aptly. He was contentious with other members of the group and had a rather bad temper. Neither he nor Cody had the discipline necessary to run the operation, preferring to spend time drinking rather than managing. Cody's assessment of the situation was that "the enterprise was not a complete financial success during the first season, though everywhere our performances were attended by immense audiences." After six months touring, the troupe returned to Omaha and Cody and Carver split up.[11]

Buffalo Bill used Winchesters exclusively for his exhibition shooting in the *Wild West*. He used his nickel-plated .44-caliber Winchester 1873 in the show.

Buffalo Bill was not on the bill for exhibition shooting when Cody and Carver's show opened in Omaha in 1883. But during Doc Carver's performance, which was not going well, the crowd shouted, "Buffalo Bill, Buffalo Bill!" Cody grabbed a rifle and proceeded to effectively dispatch a series of glass target balls. From that point on, feats of marksmanship by Buffalo Bill became a permanent part of the show.

BUFFALO BILL'S WILD WEST
AND CONGRESS OF ROUGH RIDERS OF THE WORLD.

BUFFALO BILL SHOOTING ON HORSEBACK AT FULL S...

In 1884, Buffalo Bill found a new partner, one who had the necessary show business background and managerial expertise. Two years earlier Cody had discussed the idea of a western show with Nate Salsbury, a well-known actor and impresario, but had decided to combine with Carver instead. On the heels of his split with Carver, Cody went back to Salsbury. Together they set about organizing a larger and more carefully run operation, which they renamed *Buffalo Bill's Wild West*. Guided by Buffalo Bill, celebrity and visionary, Nate Salsbury, manager and financial wizard, and John Burke, publicist extraordinaire, the *Wild West* was poised to become what Burke termed "America's National Entertainment."

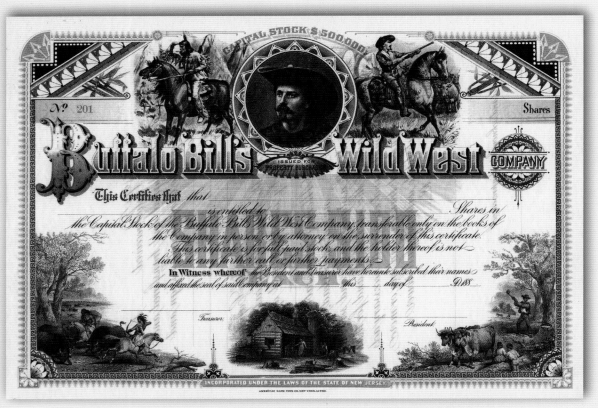

In preparation for the *Wild West*'s departure to England, the partners incorporated on February 26, 1887, issuing stock certificates to themselves and select friends. Some certificates, like this one, were printed but never issued.

The first photograph of the cast of *Buffalo Bill's Wild West* was taken while the *Wild West* was in Philadelphia during the summer of 1884.

This was the first program for *Buffalo Bill's Wild West*, issued in 1884, after the split with Doc Carver.

Watercolor of Buffalo Bill flanked by cowboys and Indians, created as original artwork for a *Wild West* advertising poster.

The 1884 season began in St. Louis and moved toward the northeast through Ohio and Pennsylvania. After stands in New England, it curved back around through New York and Washington, DC. While the *Wild West* was in Elmira, New York, Cody invited Mark Twain to visit. Twain was greatly pleased by the show and wrote:

> I have now seen your *Wild West* show two days in succession, and have enjoyed it thoroughly. It brought back vividly the breezy, wild life of the great plains and the Rocky Mountains and stirred me like a war song. Down to its smallest details the show is genuine—cowboys, vaqueros, Indians, stagecoach, costumes and all; it is wholly free from sham and insincerity, and the effects produced upon me by its spectacles were identical with those wrought upon me a long time ago by the same spectacles on the frontier.[12]

The comment from Mark Twain wasn't the only endorsement for the exhibition; over the years accolades poured in from generals under whom Buffalo Bill had served as well as all manner of persons who, like Twain, had seen the West that Cody undertook to portray. *Buffalo Bill's Wild West* had truly achieved the authenticity that he sought.

By October, the show was back in Ohio. Rather than concluding the season with the onset of winter, the partners decided to take the *Wild West* south. Their objective was the World's Industrial and Cotton Centennial Exposition in New Orleans. The thought was that this early World's Fair would attract enough people to the city to sustain a five-month stand through the winter. It didn't work out as planned.

Through the fall of 1884, the *Wild West* headed south through Kentucky, Tennessee, and Mississippi, playing to moderately sized crowds. Then the first disaster struck. On December 9, the riverboat carrying the *Wild West* cast, animals, and props sank in the Mississippi. The cast members barely escaped with their lives, the animals were lost, and all of the props but the Deadwood Stage sank. Cody telegrammed Salsbury, "Outfit at the bottom of the river, what do you advise?" Salsbury sent money, new animals were acquired, new props were built, and the show opened in New Orleans on December 23.[13]

The next disaster struck in the form of a streetcar strike. Once the streetcar strike was resolved, the rains began. It rained for forty-four straight days. The cotton exposition wasn't doing much better: people were staying away from New Orleans in droves. As Mardi Gras approached, Cody decided a big *Wild West* parade as part of the festivities would attract people to the show. It was sunny weather during the parade but, as soon as the *Wild West* opened to the public, the sky opened up and it poured.[14]

GRAY PHOTO
BOSTON.

ANNIE OAKLEY

Annie Oakley joined *Buffalo Bill's Wild West* in 1885, and over the next fifteen years she became almost as famous as Buffalo Bill.

After Mardi Gras, Cody wrote to Salsbury, "Fate if there is such a thing is against me. There is not one bit of use trying more, the longer we stick at this the worse off we are—the sooner we give this outfit away the better—I am thoroughly discouraged." When the *Wild West* finally left New Orleans on April 11, 1885, the show was $60,000 in debt.[15]

Fortunately, Cody and Salsbury did not get rid of the show. Spring marked a change in their fortunes. It came in the form of a diminutive twenty-five-year-old. Phoebe Ann Moses, who had adopted the stage name Annie Oakley, already had a reputation as a markswoman when she met Buffalo Bill in New Orleans. At the time, Captain Bogardus was the featured sharpshooter and the *Wild West* did not need another one. But Bogardus left after the disastrous New Orleans experience, leaving an opening. Annie joined the show within two weeks and soon became one of its most popular acts.[16]

That same year another person joined the *Wild West*, strengthening Buffalo Bill's quest for authenticity. In 1884, John Burke had unsuccessfully attempted to recruit Sitting Bull, the Lakota chief and medicine man, for the *Wild West*. Burke returned to the Standing Rock Indian Agency in the Dakotas once again in the summer of 1885. This time he was successful. When Sitting Bull learned that Annie Oakley was now performing with *Buffalo Bill's Wild West*, he agreed to join the show.

Captain Bogardus, a sharpshooter with *Buffalo Bill's Wild West*, advocated the use of clay pigeons as a humane alternative to shooting live pigeons. Beginning in 1884, Buffalo Bill made it a policy of the *Wild West* to use only clay pigeons or glass target balls for exhibition shooting. Cody took part in this tournament with Bogardus while the show was in New Orleans.

Colorful glass target balls were thrown in the air during marksmanship exhibitions at the *Wild West*. The balls were often filled with paper confetti or feathers, which would scatter in the air when the balls were shot. Concern that pieces of broken glass would lodge in the hoofs of the horses used by *Wild West* performers led to the invention of special resin target balls. The resin balls were painted white for use in night exhibitions.

55

He admired her shooting and nicknamed her Little Sure Shot. Unlike the other American Indians in the *Wild West*, Sitting Bull did not appear in reenactments of battles. Instead, he was presented as the great leader of the Lakota and one of those responsible for the Battle of Little Bighorn. Then he would ride slowly and in a dignified manner around the arena to boos in the United States and to cheers in Canada. Sitting Bull only appeared with the *Wild West* for four months, but John Burke's publicity capitalized on that brief appearance for the next three decades.[17]

Buffalo Bill regarded Sitting Bull with the admiration and annoyance that often occurs within friendships. While in Washington, Cody had his staff help Sitting Bull draft a letter to President Grover Cleveland and then accompanied him to a meeting with the president. He posed proudly with the Lakota chief for a portrait while the *Wild West* was in Montreal, and, when Sitting Bull left the show, the two exchanged gifts. But later Cody was quoted in publications of the times saying Sitting Bull was a "bad Indian" and "peevish." In this respect his relationship with Sitting Bull was not unlike the one he earlier maintained with Wild Bill Hickok. He admired them both but was annoyed by their faults, much as they may have been annoyed by his. Years later, Cody wrote of Sitting Bull that "in war his bitter opponent, in peace he won my friendship and sympathy; he

impressed me as a deep thinker; conscientious as to the proper rights to the lands of their fathers."[18]

Sitting Bull left the *Wild West* just as it was recovering from the disastrous stand in New Orleans. Even without his presence, the 1886 season proved to be a resounding success. Salsbury booked the *Wild West* at Erastina, a resort on Staten Island, for the entire season. Crowds flocked from New York and surrounding cities to see the show.

During the early years of *Buffalo Bill's Wild West*, Cody continued to operate the Combination, maintaining a full winter season of plays and the outdoor shows during the spring, summer, and fall. Even during the winter in New Orleans, the Combination performed sporadically. In the spring of 1886, forty-year-old Cody finally decided to close the Buffalo Bill Combination and concentrate all of his attentions on the *Wild West*. The last stage play featuring the Combination was on April 10 in Denver, Colorado. This was just the first finale in Denver for Cody; later it would be the scene of the demise of his *Wild West* and finally the place where his own life would end.[19]

Attendance was so good at Erastina that Cody and his partners decided to once again risk continuing through the winter season. This time they did not go south but instead booked Madison Square Garden. It was their first show in a covered space with a controlled environment. Large, creatively painted

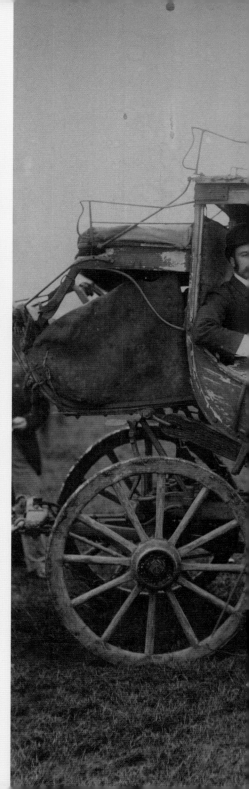

An Indian attack on the historic Deadwood Stage, with mountain man John Y. Nelson riding shotgun, was an exciting feature of the *Wild West*.

Blunted arrows, dramatically painted with red tips, were used by the American Indians during *Wild West* reenactments of battles.

Sitting Bull wore this headdress while appearing with *Buffalo Bill's Wild West*. The headdress and other Sitting Bull artifacts were featured when Johnny Baker opened the Buffalo Bill Museum in 1921.

This set of arrows and bow from Sitting Bull were acquired by the Buffalo Bill Museum from his great-grandson, Jim Blue Bird, in 1958.

Sitting Bull and Buffalo Bill posed for this publicity photo while the *Wild West* was in Montreal in 1885.

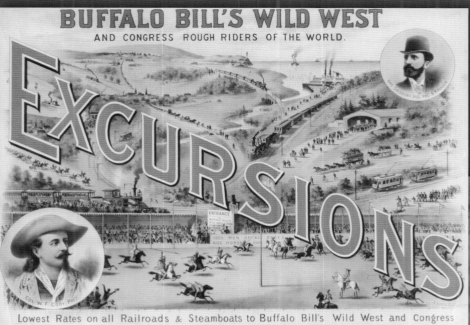

BUFFALO BILL'S WILD WEST
AND CONGRESS ROUGH RIDERS OF THE WORLD.

EXCURSIONS

COL. W.F. CODY, Pres.

Lowest Rates on all Railroads & Steamboats to Buffalo Bill's Wild West and Congress Rough Riders of the World – Exhibitions: Every Afternoon & Evening, Rain or Shine.

In the early years of *Buffalo Bill's Wild West*, the show would often stay in one place, such as the Erastina Resort on Staten Island, for an extended period. Visitors were encouraged to come from surrounding communities by whatever conveyances were available. It was not unusual for special fares to be offered to persons attending *Buffalo Bill's Wild West*.

An extended stay offered the opportunity for publicity photos to be taken of Buffalo Bill and members of his cast. This photo was taken in 1886 while the *Wild West* was performing at Erastina.

Buffalo Bill is flanked by Pawnee (on his right) and Lakota (on his left) in this publicity photo taken while at Erastina. Because of tensions between the two tribes, Cody eventually decided to have only Lakota perform in the *Wild West*.

sets were erected and wind machines installed. These preparations enabled the re-creation of everything from a primeval forest to a cyclone as *Buffalo Bill's Wild West* presented an indoor spectacle entitled "The Drama of Civilization." The new spectacle was a success, with two performances a day, each attended by as many as fifteen thousand people. The Garden became one of Cody's favorite venues, and he continued to return to it over the next twenty-five years.[20]

Between 1879 and 1883, Cody spent very little time at the family's new home in North Platte. While performing with the Combination, he was away from home from September through April or May. During the summers, he would return to North Platte for only short periods of time before heading out on hunting trips or to ranch on the Dismal River, around sixty-five miles from town. With the founding of the *Wild West*, Buffalo Bill spent even less time at home. Cody's schedule was hard on family life, and it showed. He loved spending time with his children: Orra, Arta, and Irma. Irma was the youngest, having been born in early 1883. But the initial joy of seeing his family soon disappeared as he and Louisa set into arguing. This was to become a pattern for the Codys. They fought and reconciled, and then fought and reconciled again. In 1883, Bill even considered filing for a divorce, but decided against it. The birth of daughter Irma and then, later that year, the unexpected death of their

Buffalo Bill was often away from home with the Buffalo Bill Combination during the 1870s. His relationship with his wife, Louisa, deteriorated to the point that he considered asking for a divorce in 1883.

1886 season. Cody had long dreamed of visiting Europe. After Mark Twain's visit to *Buffalo Bill's Wild West* in 1884, he urged that if the *Wild West* went to "the other side of the water" it would have the advantage of being the first distinctively American exhibition sent to England. Flush from the successes at Erastina and Madison Square Garden, Cody embarked on what he termed "an ambitious but hazardous undertaking": transporting a cast of two hundred performers plus a menagerie of wild animals across the Atlantic.[22]

middle daughter, Orra, at age eleven, may have led him to drop the idea of divorce. The Codys had lost two of their four children within the space of eight years. Besides, by that time his differences with Doc Carver were becoming irreconcilable, and he had to turn his attention to the future of the *Wild West*. After the reorganization, his visits to North Platte became even less frequent as he followed a year-round schedule with the *Wild West* and the Combination. Fewer and shorter visits home made the relationship at least bearable, and all thoughts of divorce apparently receded.[21]

Buffalo Bill's home life was furthest from his mind at the conclusion of the

The *Wild West*'s interpretation "The Drama of Civilization" played before record crowds at Madison Square Garden during the winter of 1886–87.

Chapter Five
Americans and Europeans

1887–1892

The Indian, as you know, is a pretty good man. I have never led the troops of the United States Army against the Indians that I didn't do it with a feeling of regret, because they are the original inhabitants of this country. They were driven from the Atlantic to the Pacific Ocean, backwards and forwards, and they once owned this entire country. *Buffalo Bill, 1907*

Buffalo Bill walked out of dinner. It had gone well. Everyone seemed to like the idea of a massive statue of an American Indian in New York Harbor, as tall as Lady Liberty. Liberty was a gift from the Old World to the New World, but this statue would be a gift from America to all peoples. Representing the first Americans, it would welcome immigrants just as the Pilgrims were welcomed. And it would be a bold tribute, illustrating the red man's bravery and nobility. Even old Sitting Bull might have appreciated this. Of course, the statue would have to be authentic, an Indian brave in full regalia, just like the warriors in the *Wild West*.

This poster is filled with symbols of the West, including the representation of Buffalo Bill in his role as a scout and a depiction of an American Indian as "The American."

By 1900 it was thought that, like the buffalo, American Indians would vanish. Certainly both official and unofficial policies of the US government had been aimed at first confining and then eradicating Indian culture. *Buffalo Bill's Wild West* was one of the few places where both the buffalo and Plains Indian culture were still being preserved. In 1909, Cody joined Rodman Wanamaker and other citizens in an effort to erect a statue (to be designed by Frederic Remington) in tribute to, as Cody put it, "the noble qualities of the Indian." While the statue never came to fruition, Cody's involvement in the project was a result of his ongoing effort to present the culture of his former foes.[1]

Buffalo Bill's Wild West represented Indians as the original Americans. Advertising posters for the show frequently included the visage of an American Indian with the title "The American." A man of his times, Cody felt that white man's civilization was superior and the original Americans had to make way for it. But at the same time, he admired the Indians' culture and advocated for their rights. He had little trouble recruiting them to be part of his *Wild West*. There was little resentment held against him by his former foes, whom he always treated honorably. It was a simple proposition for both parties: they had been enemies, and now they weren't. Participation in the *Wild West* gave American Indians an opportunity to leave the reservation, earn money, and preserve a culture that was being taken away from them.

As Cody and his partners prepared for their visit to Europe, they kept American Indians central to the show and its advertising. They were the most important part of *Buffalo Bill's Wild West*; few of the people who attended the show in the States had ever seen an Indian. Even fewer Europeans had seen one, although everyone had heard about them. The challenge was getting the American Indians across the Atlantic.

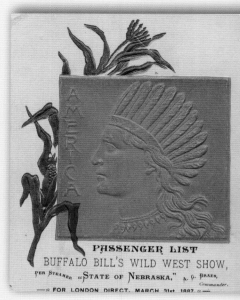

The presence of American Indians performing feats of horsemanship and interpreting their culture was critical to the success of the *Wild West*.

"Our arrangements having at length been completed, by collecting together a company of more than two hundred men and animals, consisting of Indians, cowboys (including the celebrated Cowboy Band), Mexican wild riders, celebrated rifle shots, buffaloes, Texas steers, burros, broncos, racing horses, elk, bears, and an immense amount of camp paraphernalia, such as tents, wagons, stage coach, etc., we chartered the steamship *State of Nebraska*, of the State line, Capt. Braes, and were ready to set sail to a country that I had long wished to visit—the Motherland." —Buffalo Bill, 1888

Some thought that if they crossed the ocean, they would die. When the steamship *State of Nebraska* left New York Harbor on March 31, 1887, there was a contingent of Indians aboard, having been successfully persuaded that there was nothing to fear. That fear returned as many onboard experienced seasickness. But when the ship reached England on April 16, no lives had been lost and the spirits of all were raised.[2]

Buffalo Bill's Wild West visited England as part of the Golden Jubilee celebration of the reign of Queen Victoria. It was just one part of an American Exposition organized for the occasion but quickly became the feature attraction. In fact, as Mark Twain predicted, it was the first time that Londoners had experienced something that was truly from America. Not only did crowds flock to the *Wild West*, London society clamored to host the visitors. Cody attended tea with Oscar Wilde, partied with famed actor Henry Irving, and dined with the Churchills (whose young son Winston later attended the show). Lakota chief Red Shirt, an articulate and handsome warrior, was particularly popular. Red Shirt accompanied Buffalo Bill to many

A view of the *Wild West* at Earl's Court in London, May 7, 1887.

Colonel Cody

Mr. & Mrs. Oscar Wilde
at Home
Wednesday July 13.
4—7.
16 Tite Street
Chelsea   *R.S.V.P.*

Monday

My dear Sir
Have you any evening engagement for Saturday next, the 9.? The Prince of Wales is doing me the honour of coming here to supper at about 11.30, & I should be very glad if you would come &...

The toast of London in 1887, Buffalo Bill was invited to tea with Oscar Wilde and supper with the Prince of Wales.

parties, as well as to Parliament. Also accompanying Cody to parties was his twenty-one-year-old daughter, Arta, whom he later took on a two-week vacation to Italy. Arta remained with her father throughout the show's stay in England.[3]

Buffalo Bill wrote, "I am convinced—and I say it in no boastful spirit—that our visit to England has set the population of the British Islands reading, thinking and talking about their American kinsman to an extent before unprecedented." *Buffalo Bill's Wild West* attracted all strata of London citizenry, from the working class to the aristocracy. Special performances were given to the Prince and Princess of Wales, as well as to Queen Victoria herself. Cody was particularly proud of the command performance before the queen. He wrote that she saluted the American flag for the first time in history, and he felt that acknowledgment, as well as the positive manner in which the *Wild West* was received in England, was a diplomatic victory.[4]

Following five months of performances at Earl's Court in London, the *Wild West* moved on to Birmingham and then Manchester. There Cody presented a camp dinner of Maryland chicken, Boston pork and beans, rib roast, corn cakes, and other American foods to dignitaries and the press. Farewell dinners as well as Fourth of July dinners would become common during the *Wild West*'s tours of Europe and the United States.[5]

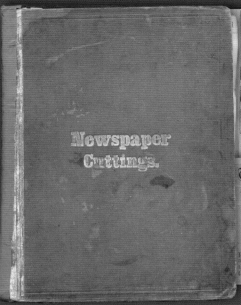

This book of clippings was one of twenty-five kept by Buffalo Bill during the *Wild West*'s 1887 to 1892 visits to Europe.

Buffalo Bill posed for this publicity photograph in London in 1887.

Johnny Baker · John Nelson · Jule Keen · Mjr. Burke · Buck Taylor · Buffalo Bill.

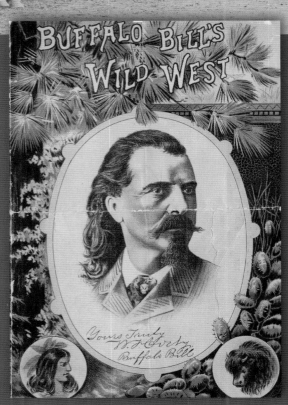

BUFFALO BILL'S
WILD WEST

Yours Truly
W.F. Cody
Buffalo Bill

In this drawing of the American Exhibition in London (above), the circular arena of *Buffalo Bill's Wild West* can be seen to the right of the main exhibition building.

This program (left and top), including an attack on the Deadwood Stage, was first used in 1887. The inside information was translated to French when the *Wild West* appeared at the Exposition Universelle in Paris in 1889.

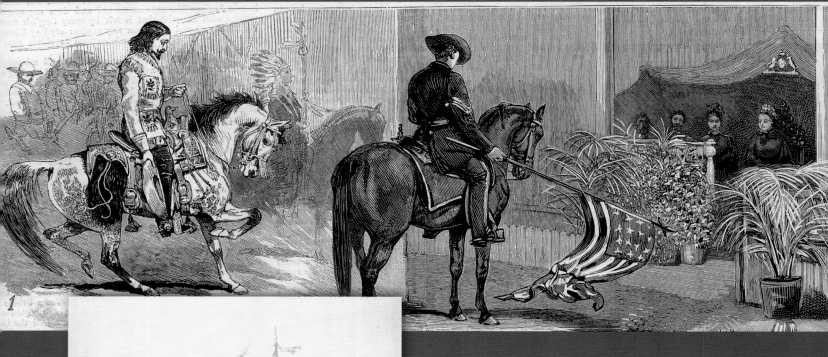

After the successes in London in 1886, particularly the command performance for the queen, Cody had this poster created. It featured a quotation from the London *Times*: "Buffalo Bill has done his part in bringing America and England together."

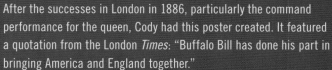

The *Wild West* held a large dinner of American cuisine for the press and dignitaries in Manchester, England, in 1888. This event was so successful that special celebratory dinners, often featuring buffalo and other American specialties, became a *Wild West* tradition.

Buffalo Bill kept this scrapbook of invitations to parties and social events during his 1892 visit to England.

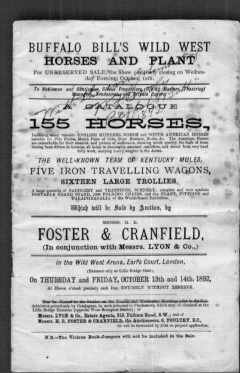

When the *Wild West* returned to America in 1892, part of the show was sold at auction in London. This included tepees, painted backdrops, horses, and the four mules that had pulled the Deadwood Stage during the show's nearly six years in Europe. This bill for the auction was signed, "With the compliments of W. F. Cody Buffalo Bill 1892."

A Far Eastern Artist's idea of Buffalo Bill

COL.W.F.CODY
"BUFFALO BILL"

The depiction of Buffalo Bill using symbols of the West was created in 1892 by English artist Alick P. F. Ritchie. It was used on several *Wild West* posters, including this version from 1910. It stands in marked contrast to the portrait of a more heroic Cody by American artist Henry Atwell Thomas, created in 1888 and reproduced on this poster by A. Hoen and Company.

These caricatures in popular magazines of the period, although not always complimentary, were testimony to the fascination of the European media with the *Wild West*, particularly the American Indians.

On May 5, 1888, *Buffalo Bill's Wild West* returned to the United States. It was an uneventful journey, with no mention of seasickness. There was one loss, which Cody noted with great sadness. His horse Charley, whom he had ridden for fifteen years and who had even been profiled in London papers, died during the journey and was given a traditional burial at sea. The ship, the *Persian Monarch*, landed on Staten Island so that the show could be taken to Erastina. Erastina, where the *Wild West* had performed two years earlier, would be the site of the first performances upon the show's return.

Red Shirt, Tall Horse, Kills Plenty, and the other Lakota clung to the ship's rails as it pulled into the harbor, pleased with their adventure but glad to be home. Some would stay in Erastina while others returned to the plains. The season finished in Richmond, Virginia, after touring through several states. The Indians who stayed with Cody joined him and other members of the *Wild West* at a special reception with President Cleveland in the White House. After the reception, Buffalo Bill and the cast returned to their homes in the West.

Cody, now an international sensation, made a triumphant return to North Platte and began several months of socializing and ceremony. Just before leaving for England, William Cody had been commissioned as a colonel and aide-de-camp in the Nebraska National Guard by Governor John M. Thayer. Thayer was reelected just after Cody's return to Nebraska. As the governor's aide-de-camp and, more importantly, as Nebraska's biggest celebrity, Cody was caught up in victory celebrations and the inaugural festivities. For a time, he and Louisa were on good terms.[6]

The winter of 1888 through 1889 concluded, and the *Wild West* returned to Europe, this time to tour the Continent. Despite the disastrous stand in New Orleans during the cotton exposition a few years earlier, Cody and Salsbury felt their luck had changed with the success they experienced at the American Exposition in London. They decided to go to Paris for the Exposition Universelle, a six-month centennial celebration of the French Revolution.

Once again, *Buffalo Bill's Wild West* was in the right place at the right time. It came to represent all that was unique about America, just as it had in London. John Burke made sure that the uniqueness was front and center. A report from the exhibition stated that "the immense painted posters over all the city to advertise Buffalo Bill—his portraits pasted all in a row, many times larger than natural; the cowboys on their wild horses; the Indians, looking very savage—amuse the Parisians immensely. It is something new."[7]

The *Wild West* opened in Paris to an audience of thousands, including French president Marie François Sadi Carnot. Every day for the next six months, the arena, which seated fifteen thousand people, was nearly full for both afternoon and evening shows. Parisians were particularly fascinated by the Indians, whose ranks had swelled to 102. One Parisian who attended the *Wild West* numerous times was well-known French artist Rosa Bonheur, who painted the Indians and the animals in the *Wild West*. Her efforts culminated in a portrait of Buffalo Bill mounted on his white horse Tucker.[8]

A high point, both literally and figuratively, of the Paris trip for the American Indians was a visit to the Eiffel Tower on Bastille Day, a month after the tower's grand opening. They followed the lead of thousands of Parisians, as well as the president of France, the Prince of Wales, the king of Siam, Thomas Edison…and Buffalo Bill. *Wild West* publicist John Burke took the Indians to the top of the tower. Some, like Red Shirt, had been in elevators during their previous trip to England. But none had experienced elevators like those on the Eiffel Tower. And none had ever been on such a tall structure. They were awed by the view.[9]

The European tour of the *Wild West* was inspiring for all parties. As the *Wild West* toured the rest of France, Spain, and Italy, its cast was exposed to new wonders at every stop. These ranged from Roman ruins like the Colosseum to the massive cathedrals of Germany. The *Wild West* even held a performance in the ancient coliseum at Verona. The people of Europe were equally fascinated by the members of the *Wild West*. Cowboy hats became a fashion rage, and the show may even have inspired the great composer Giacomo Puccini to write an opera about the West. In Germany, visitors flocked to the *Wild West*. They were particularly fascinated by the life and costumes of the Indians.[10]

The *Wild West* staged a performance in the ancient coliseum of Verona during the show's 1890 visit to Italy.

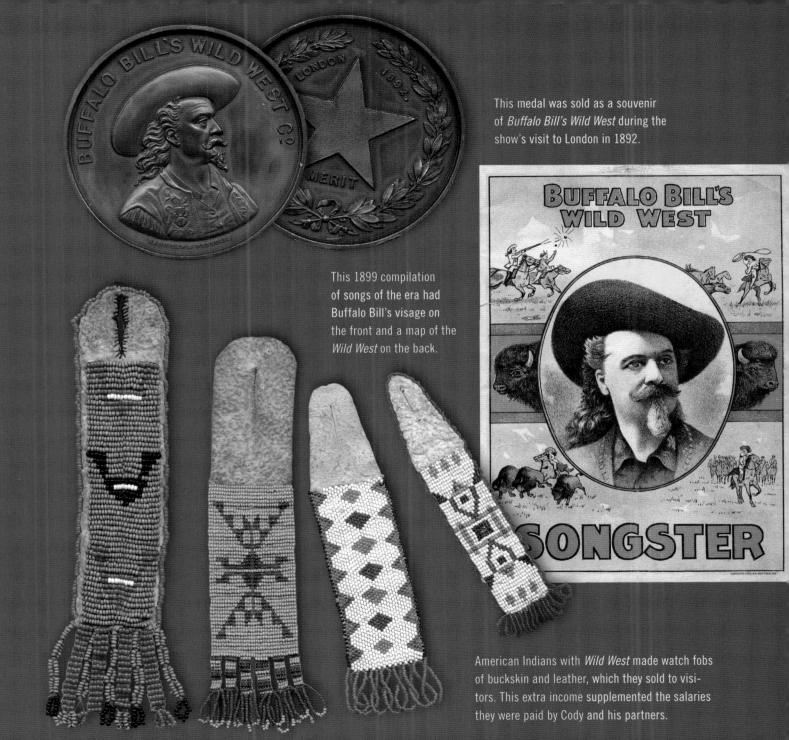

This medal was sold as a souvenir of *Buffalo Bill's Wild West* during the show's visit to London in 1892.

This 1899 compilation of songs of the era had Buffalo Bill's visage on the front and a map of the *Wild West* on the back.

American Indians with *Wild West* made watch fobs of buckskin and leather, which they sold to visitors. This extra income supplemented the salaries they were paid by Cody and his partners.

In 1898, Parker Brothers introduced *Buffalo Bill*, a board game that took Cody on a scouting adventure with threats of capture by Indians and a buffalo stampede.

This cap gun, made by the Stevens Company in 1890, capitalized on the Buffalo Bill name.

Sets of six die cuts, each illustrating a different *Wild West* scene, were made and sold in Europe during the early 1900s.

This children's pop-up book was published in Stuttgart, Germany, in 1891.

In 1887, McLoughlin Brothers of New York published this booklet with a long, illustrated poem about a visit to the *Wild West*.

Rosa Bonheur painted a portrait of Buffalo Bill on his horse Tucker while the *Wild West* was in Paris in 1889. In 1898, that portrait became the subject of a *Wild West* poster that contrasted an alert and heroic Cody with a slouching, lackluster Napoleon. Buffalo Bill Historical Center, Cody, Wyoming, Given in memory of William R. Coe and Mai Rogers Coe, 8.66.

While Cody recognized the publicity value of being painted by Rosa Bonheur, he was not particularly happy with the way he was depicted in the painting. He later asked Robert Lindneux to create a duplicate of the Bonheur painting, but with softer features. That painting was then the basis for several *Wild West* advertising posters.

This poster-sized bas-relief carving of Cody (below), created by W. C. DeWitt, was based on the Lindneux version of Bonheur's painting.

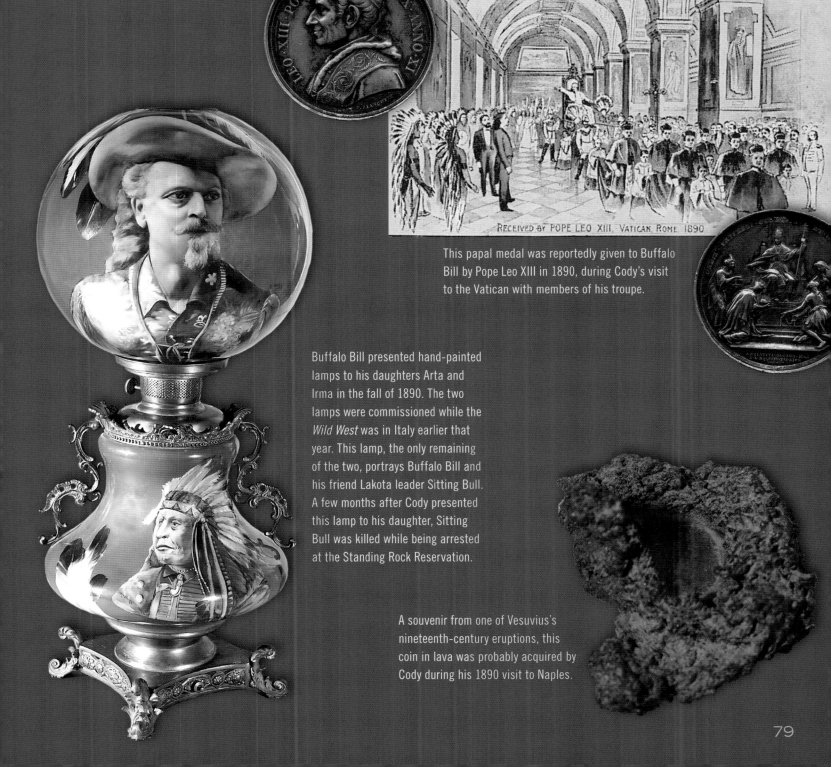

RECEIVED BY POPE LEO XIII, VATICAN, ROME 1890

This papal medal was reportedly given to Buffalo Bill by Pope Leo XIII in 1890, during Cody's visit to the Vatican with members of his troupe.

Buffalo Bill presented hand-painted lamps to his daughters Arta and Irma in the fall of 1890. The two lamps were commissioned while the *Wild West* was in Italy earlier that year. This lamp, the only remaining of the two, portrays Buffalo Bill and his friend Lakota leader Sitting Bull. A few months after Cody presented this lamp to his daughter, Sitting Bull was killed while being arrested at the Standing Rock Reservation.

A souvenir from one of Vesuvius's nineteenth-century eruptions, this coin in lava was probably acquired by Cody during his 1890 visit to Naples.

Buffalo Bill's Wild West played Naples for almost a month in 1890. During this time, Vesuvius experienced some minor volcanic activity, which could be seen from the *Wild West* camp. Later, after a more severe eruption, in 1906, Cody made a contribution of $5,000 to relief efforts. This certificate from the Italian government recognized him for his contribution.

A highlight of the continental tour occurred in early 1890, when Buffalo Bill and his company attended an audience held by Pope Leo XIII. Publicist John Burke briefed the company on the appropriate protocol for the visit. He later wrote, "The grandeur of the spectacle, the heavenly music, the entrancing singing, and the impressive adjuncts produced a most profound impression on the astonished children of the prairie."[11]

While the Lakota were impressed by the sights, they grew homesick and wanted to return to the plains. There were also problems brewing back home that gave Cody reason to send them back to the States. Following the 1890 summer season, Cody set up a camp in Europe for the rest of the troupe and sent the Indians on a ship to Philadelphia. The problems were waiting on the gangplank when the ship pulled into the harbor.

While the show was in Europe, a loosely networked group of missionaries, Indian Bureau commissioners, and other individuals who felt the American

These photographs of Buffalo Bill were taken in Paris during the *Wild West*'s 1890 tour of Europe.

Indians should be kept on the reservations had organized. These reformers, whose primary concern was the "civilizing" of the Indians by repressing their culture, accused Cody and his partners of mistreating the Indians in their care. The *Wild West* Indians, however, testified that they had been treated well, paid well, and had enjoyed their travels. Four had died in Spain during an outbreak of typhoid fever, but so had other performers. Ironically, the death rate on the reservation, where the reformers sought to confine them, was much higher. After a series of hearings, the partners were exonerated. But the *Wild West* continued to be criticized well into the twentieth century because it allowed American Indians to retain their culture and re-create it for show visitors. Some of the criticism came from the Carlisle School in Pennsylvania, which sought to assimilate Indians and had a stated mission to "kill the Indian and save the man."[12]

As Buffalo Bill and his group of 102 headed eastward to France in 1889, another smaller group of American Indians had begun a westward journey. By that time most people in the United States, including the government, thought the Indian Wars were over. In one respect they were correct: the military might of the Plains Indians had been crushed. But mistreatment, poverty, and broken promises had led the original Americans to look for something new. That search led them to a messiah.

During 1889, word came to the Lakota that a Paiute Indian by the name of Wovoka was having visions and had been told by God that a new age would come. Wovoka, as God's messenger and a new messiah, preached a doctrine of peace and faithfulness. Followers were not to fight the white man but were to find ways to accommodate white society. A sign of their faithfulness would be a special dance performed by the followers, a Ghost Dance. This religious movement, with many strong connections to Christianity, was pan-Indian in its intent and scope. Tribes that had been enemies were to be at peace with each other as well as with the white man.[13]

The Lakota selected ten representatives to travel to Nevada, where they would meet Wovoka and learn about this new religious movement. As the delegation moved westward, they were joined by representatives from other tribes, including the Shoshone, the Arapaho, and the Bannock, all seeking to learn more about the messiah. Among the Lakota was Short Bull, who had been a warrior as a youth and now, in middle age, had become a medicine man. Short Bull met Wovoka and was touched by his message. Upon the delegation's return from Nevada, Short Bull was threatened by members of the reservation's Indian police, who felt the Ghost Dance would be disruptive. Despite this, he became a leader of the Ghost Dance among the Lakota.[14]

Short Bull and his wife with Johnny Baker (on the left) and Mr. and Mrs. V. R. Day. Day was the general manager of the Essanay Film Company, which worked with Buffalo Bill on a film about the Indian Wars in 1913. This photograph was probably taken while filming a re-creation of the Battle at Wounded Knee.

This *Wild West* poster shows Buffalo Bill assisting the Nebraska National Guard and the US Army in the aftermath of Wounded Knee. Ghost Dance leader Short Bull joined the *Wild West* and later gave Johnny Baker his headdress, canvas coat decorated with a battle scene, and a dew-claw necklace (right).

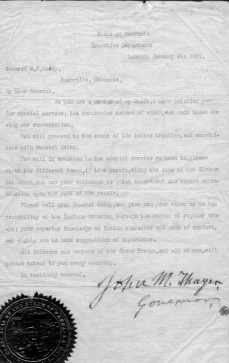

In 1892, while traveling with *Buffalo Bill's Wild West* through England, Short Bull told the story of his involvement with the Ghost Dance to George Crager, a translator with the show. Crager wrote down this eyewitness account, including Short Bull's memories of Wounded Knee, and it is a primary source of information about the Ghost Dance.

In 1889, Governor John M. Thayer of Nebraska increased Buffalo Bill's commission with the National Guard to that of general. He later asked him to work with General Nelson Miles and the Nebraska State Troopers monitoring the unrest after Wounded Knee.

The Ghost Dance as preached by Wovoka and as practiced by the Lakota was a peaceful movement. But to the Indian agents, Indian commissioners, and settlements surrounding the reservations, it was a threat. They felt that anything that empowered American Indians and united them was dangerous, even if it preached peace. So the Office of Indian Affairs banned the Ghost Dance. As far as the US government was concerned, anything the Indians did that rejected governmental authority was to be considered hostile. At the same time, there were extremists among the American Indians who favored armed resistance and felt giving up the Ghost Dance was an unacceptable accommodation. The Ghost Dancers soon found themselves caught between two factions: tribal extremists and the United States government.[15]

Buffalo Bill returned to the United States from Europe in late 1890 to find the Ghost Dance in full swing and tensions mounting. His intention had been to counter the charges of the reformers and testify about the good treatment of American Indians under his charge. Instead he found himself drawn into the conflict over the Ghost Dance. His old friend and commander, General Nelson Miles, concerned that Sitting Bull was behind the growing unrest, requested that Cody proceed to the Standing Rock Reservation and take Sitting Bull into custody. Cody invited several friends who had also known Sitting Bull in 1885 to join him in the effort. He also took gifts, including sweets, a particular favorite of Sitting Bull. Cody was clearly more interested in persuading Sitting Bull to accompany him than in arresting the Lakota chief.[16]

The unarmed party proceeded toward Sitting Bull's camp but was intercepted by a message from President Benjamin Harrison. The president had been persuaded by the Indian commissioners, and by Indian agent James McLaughlin in particular, that Buffalo Bill should not perform the task. A few days later, General Miles sent a letter to Cody explaining that the mission had been thwarted by McLaughlin and stating that he did not agree with the agent's action. Ten days later, Sitting Bull was dead, shot by the reservation's Indian police when, under orders from McLaughlin, they attempted to arrest him.[17]

While he was certainly not a central figure in the Ghost Dance, Sitting Bull's death on December 18, 1890, marked the beginning of the end for the movement. The US government began a crackdown on the Ghost Dancers that led to an outright massacre of men, women, and children at Wounded Knee on December 29. Short Bull later recalled that he came upon the battlefield to discover twenty-three of his relatives had died. Nevertheless, he tried to focus upon the peaceful teachings of Wovoka and not allow himself to be overcome by anger.[18]

One of Sitting Bull's two wives is shown here in her cabin on the reservation after Sitting Bull's death. According to Johnny Baker's records, this elk tooth dress (right) belonged to her.

HEADQUARTERS DIVISION OF THE MISSOURI,

CHICAGO, ILL., December 4th, 1890.8

Colonel W.F.Cody,

Dear Colonel:-

Your report dated LaCrosse, Wisconsin, December 3rd, is at hand. I regret that you did not accomplish the object of your mission, but it was, however, not through any fault of yours. On the representation of Agent McLaughlin that in his opinion the arrest of a certain Indian would precepitate hostilities, the President gave the order to suspend the arrest. I do not concur in the opinion of the Agent.

I appreciate the energy, spirit and fortitude of your undertaking, and realized that you would enter into the work the same as you have in other hazardous service.

Very Truly Yours

Nelson A Miles

Major General

Com'dg

Confidential

HEADQUARTERS DIVISION OF THE MISSOURI,

CHICAGO, ILL., Nov 24 1890.

Col Cody

You are hereby authorized to secure the person of Sitting Bull and and deliver him to the nearest comdg officer of U.S. troops

taking a receipt and reporting your action.

Nelson A Miles

Major Gen

Comdg Div

General Miles's note asking Buffalo Bill to bring in Sitting Bull, and his letter of apology after Cody was prevented from doing so.

According to Johnny Baker's records, this peace pipe belonged to Sitting Bull.

On January 6, 1890, Buffalo Bill received a letter from Governor Thayer of Nebraska asking him to work with General Miles of the US Army and the Nebraska state troopers on the "Indian troubles." By this time, those troubles were almost over. Ten days after Cody's appointment, the leaders of the Ghost Dance surrendered. Buffalo Bill was present with his friend General Miles. The nineteen leaders were taken as prisoners to Fort Sheridan in Illinois. There they posed a problem for the army, which was under pressure to release them but did not want to return them to the reservation, fearing they would revive the Ghost Dance. Buffalo Bill offered a solution. The Ghost Dancers could come with the *Wild West* to Europe in the spring. All but four of the leaders joined the *Wild West*, taking sixty of their friends and relatives with them.[19]

Cody's partner Nate Salsbury, who had stayed in Europe when Burke, Cody, and the Lakota returned to the States, was worried that the reformers would win and the American Indian contingent would have to be dropped from the show altogether. During the winter, Salsbury focused his creative energies on coming up with a way to replace the Indians if that became necessary. The result was a new direction and name for the show: *Buffalo Bill's Wild West and Congress of Rough Riders of the World*. The show would feature international horsemen and horsewomen demonstrating their

skills. The cowboys, with whom the term *rough rider* originated, would be joined by South American gauchos, Cossacks, English lancers, and others.[20]

Over the next two years, *Buffalo Bill's Wild West and Congress of Rough Riders of the World* toured Germany and Belgium, then returned to England, Scotland, and Wales. Throughout the tour, the Ghost Dancers were well treated and well fed. Short Bull said, "If our people have any complaints it is fixed at once." He also remarked that he really liked the English people but did not care for their rainy weather. In the fall of 1892, the show returned to the United States, where it would have the most successful season in its history.[21]

Chapter Six

Rough Riding to Riches
1893–1904

Great Scott, these Chicago real estate men simply want the earth. Their prices are fabulous and I don't see how I can meet their terms, but I'm going to try to locate our show somewhere in Chicago. *Buffalo Bill, 1893*

This poster, printed in 1894, used the European tours of the *Wild West* to enhance the credibility of the show to potential visitors. The poster's title, "From Prairie to Palace," was also the title of a promotional book published the year before by John Burke.

The dinner was over, and speeches honoring Deputy Consul-General Edmund J. Moffat had begun. Buffalo Bill's mind wandered. How things had changed in just a decade. At one time he had been a curiosity to society, someone you might invite to a party to show off to your friends, but not someone who was considered an equal. But now people were approaching him for counsel and support. These men at the table were Buffalo Bill's peers; he was not just a novelty to them. He was surrounded by the leading lights of London: doctors, lawyers, politicians, and even artists. Renowned British artist Solomon J. Solomon was seated to his right, and James McNeill Whistler was at the next table. Cody finally had the acclaim that he had pursued for so many years.[1]

By the time he celebrated his forty-seventh birthday in 1893, Buffalo Bill had achieved a status attained by few others in his time. The successes in New York and Europe had made him one of the best-known persons of his time.

Because of his experience during the Indian Wars, he was consulted on issues of military significance, and with the *Wild West* as a financial success, he was sought out as a leading businessman. Not only was his fame growing, he was beginning to amass a fortune.

Will Cody always had a restless mind. From that moment in his youth when he saw the westward-bound wagons, like ships departing for parts unknown, he sought new horizons. Buffalo hunting, scouting, the Combination, the *Wild West*, all had been part of his quest for new possibilities. Now, after surviving the rigors of both frontier and civilized life, he was in his prime. He could follow in his father's footsteps by being a town founder and advocating for just causes. He also had the money to try new ventures.

There was a great new opportunity awaiting the *Wild West* in Chicago. The city was planning an exposition. It would celebrate the discovery of the New World by Christopher Columbus and would be the largest exposition of its kind. *Buffalo Bill's Wild West* had been a success at the American Exposition in London and at the Exposition Universelle in Paris. As far as Buffalo Bill, Nate Salsbury, and John Burke were concerned, the now-expanded *Buffalo Bill's Wild West and Congress of Rough Riders of the World* was on its way to Chicago. Unfortunately, the Ways and Means Committee of the World's Columbian

Exposition didn't see things the same way and rejected their request to be part of the fair's midway. Undeterred, the partners looked for land elsewhere. They finally purchased fifteen acres opposite the fair's entrance. It was costly, but turned out to be one of the partners' shrewdest business moves.

When the World's Columbian Exposition opened on May 1, 1893, *Buffalo Bill's Wild West and Congress of Rough Riders of the World* had already been operating for one month. Able to accommodate eighteen thousand people for each show, it was playing to sell-out crowds. Even on the exposition's opening day, the *Wild West* had to turn people away.[2]

This aerial view of the *Wild West*, with the Ferris wheel in the background, shows its close proximity to the 1893 World's Columbian Exposition. The entrances to the *Wild West* and the exposition were virtually next to each other.

However, there were some people whom Buffalo Bill couldn't bear to turn away. When the exposition's officials refused to provide a day of free admission to the poor children of the city, Buffalo Bill sponsored a "waif's day" with free food and admission to his show. Fifteen thousand children attended. This wasn't out of the ordinary for Cody; for years he had been providing free admission to the residents of orphanages. But the people of Chicago were impressed with this generosity. The subsequent publicity in local newspapers drove even more people to the *Wild West*. [3]

Unlike the World's Columbian Exposition, the *Wild West* was open on Sundays. After suffragist Susan B. Anthony commented that if she had a son, she thought he would learn more at the *Wild West* than in church, Buffalo

Bill extended complimentary box tickets to her. The day that she attended, he rode over and gave a deep bow. This was also the first public gesture of support by Cody for women's suffrage. His opinion on the issue was later expressed in an 1899 program for the *Wild West*, where he not only said that women should be able to vote but advocated that they be given equal rights: "What we want to do is give our women even more liberty than they have. Let them do any kind of work that they see fit, and if they do it as well as men give them the same pay." He continued to express this opinion for the rest of his life. In an interview a few months before his death, he said his support of women's rights was motivated by his love for his "dear mother." [4]

Buffalo Bill's Wild West and Congress of Rough Riders of the World struck an insidious blow for equal rights for women. Cowgirls in split skirts rode as equals to cowboys, and female Cossacks exhibited skills identical to those of the males. A popular event during the show was a horse race between women from three backgrounds: Anglo, Spanish, and Indian. Annie Oakley bested all challengers, male or female, at marksmanship. Oakley in particular, with her very proper Victorian clothing, showed that a woman could retain her femininity and still compete with men on the masculine plane.

Cowgirls in the *Wild West* exhibited riding skills that were equal to those of the cowboys.

The 1893 appearance of *Buffalo Bill's Wild West* opposite the main entrance to the World's Columbian Exposition netted over a million dollars for Cody and his partners.

These companion posters would have been more expensive to produce than regular advertising posters and were probably sold as *Wild West* souvenirs in Chicago in 1893, as was the commemorative candy dish.

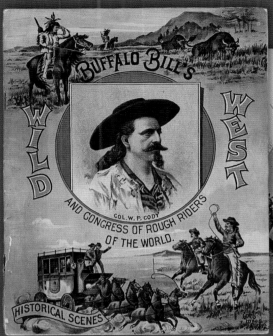

The exposition occasionally sponsored special days, like Manhattan Day, for special groups. When the fair's managers reneged on a promise to sponsor a free admission day for local orphans, Buffalo Bill sponsored his own "waif's day" with food and free admission. A local paper carried the headline "Bravo! Buffalo Bill. He Entertained Chicago's Poverty-Stricken Children When the Haughty Fair Directors Refused Them Admission."

The Russian Cossacks, actually Gurian riders from Georgia, demonstrated feats of horsemanship while carrying knives in their teeth and swinging swords overhead (below).

Rough riders in London in 1892, illustrated by Frederic Remington (above).

BUFFALO BILL'S WILD WEST.
CONGRESS, ROUGH RIDERS OF THE WORLD.

JOHNNIE BAKER,
THE MARVELOUS MARKSMAN.

BUFFALO BILL'S WILD WEST.
CONGRESS, ROUGH RIDERS OF THE WORLD

MISS ANNIE OAKLEY,
THE PEERLESS LADY WING-SHOT.

BUFFALO BILL'S WILD WEST.
AND CONGRESS OF ROUGH RIDERS.

SOUTH AMERICAN GAUCHOS.
FIRST EVER SEEN IN THE UNITED STATES.
BY PERMISSION OF THE ARGENTINE GOVERNMENT.

BUFFALO BILL'S WILD WEST.
AND CONGRESS OF ROUGH RIDERS.

RUSSIAN COSSACKS.
FOR THE FIRST TIME IN AMERICA.
BY PERMISSION OF THE CZAR.

Will. House,
SWORD & LANCE EXPERT,
and Rough Rider,
Season 1899.   Buffalo Bill's Wild West.

Edward Gallagher,
U. S. CAVALRY.
BUFFALO BILL'S WILD WEST.
Season 1899.

This business-card holder belonged to an English lancer, William House. It also held a business card from US Cavalry rider Edward Gallagher. As the cards indicate, both rode with the *Wild West*'s rough riders during the 1899 season.

A series of posters depicting different rough riders and other characters with the *Wild West* was created by A. Hoen and Company of Baltimore for advertising the show while it appeared in Chicago in 1893.

While in Chicago, the rough riders of the world came into their own as a major dimension of the show. Audiences unfamiliar with gauchos, Arabians, and Cossacks saw them for the first time, performing feats of horsemanship. Such minor details as the fact that the Cossacks weren't Cossacks at all, but were instead Gurians from the country of Georgia, didn't bother them a bit. The audiences were simply thrilled to see the rough riding, which included races between the different ethnic groups.[5]

The season of 1893, from April through October, proved to be the *Wild West*'s best. Not only was the World's Columbian Exposition one of the most popular and financially successful world fairs ever held, the show's placement opposite its entrance was perfect. A visit to the *Wild West* became as important as a visit to the exposition. By October, the show had been visited by 4 million people and the partners' profits were in the neighborhood of a million dollars.[6]

This 1895 booklet was distributed in towns before the arrival of *Buffalo Bill's Wild West and Congress of Rough Riders of the World.* The cover shows the various groups that were part of the rough riders, as well as Buffalo Bill and Nate Salsbury.

All of these items were worn by Buffalo Bill in the *Wild West* during the late 1890s.

Buffalo Bill returned to North Platte from Chicago filled with generosity. He had always been an openhanded man, and with his newfound wealth he expanded his giving. When his train arrived, he was welcomed home by most of the town, including a brass band. He immediately decided the band members needed uniforms and ordered some from Chicago. The uniforms were the finest anyone in town had seen and included a photo button of Buffalo Bill on the front. He made contributions to every church in town and various civic organizations. Old friends and family members also experienced windfalls from Cody's good fortune. He even purchased his wife, Louisa, a new house, a local mansion they nicknamed Welcome Wigwam.[7]

In 1886, Cody had purchased a ranch outside North Platte and built a second home on it. It was near enough to town to be convenient, and yet far enough away to provide him, on his infrequent visits, with an occasionally necessary retreat from Louisa. Scout's Rest Ranch, managed by his sister Julia and her husband, received an infusion of capital after Cody's return from Chicago. It was soon considered one of the finest purebred cattle and horse ranches in western Nebraska.[8]

Now that he had money to invest, Cody expanded his interests from show business and ranching into other areas. He joined old friend Dr. Frank Powell of La Crosse, Wisconsin, in manufacturing a coffee substitute called Panamilt. That venture lasted about a year before failing. It wasn't the first or last of Cody's business ventures to fail.[9]

Historians of the West often look upon 1893 as a pivotal year. In 1890, the US Census had essentially declared that there was no longer an American frontier. During a meeting of the American Historical Association in Chicago, an event linked to the World's Columbian Exposition, Frederick Jackson Turner reiterated that information. He stated that after four hundred years of history beginning with Christopher Columbus, America had finished with its frontier period and was entering a new era. As Turner addressed the assembled historians, in another part of town Buffalo Bill was welcoming visitors to his *Wild West*, a vestige of that frontier. But, just as Buffalo Bill had played a part in the passing of the American frontier, he wanted to play a part in the creation of a new America.

"Back to the New West, the Wild West I leave with you," Cody wrote on a publicity flyer in 1911. After the financial success of the *Wild West* in 1893, Cody increasingly turned his attentions toward investing in the future. By 1911, a list of his business involvements included a housing addition in North Platte, five mining and oil companies in Arizona and Wyoming, five farms, two large ranches for the raising of purebred horses and cattle, land in Minnesota and Wisconsin, three hotels outside

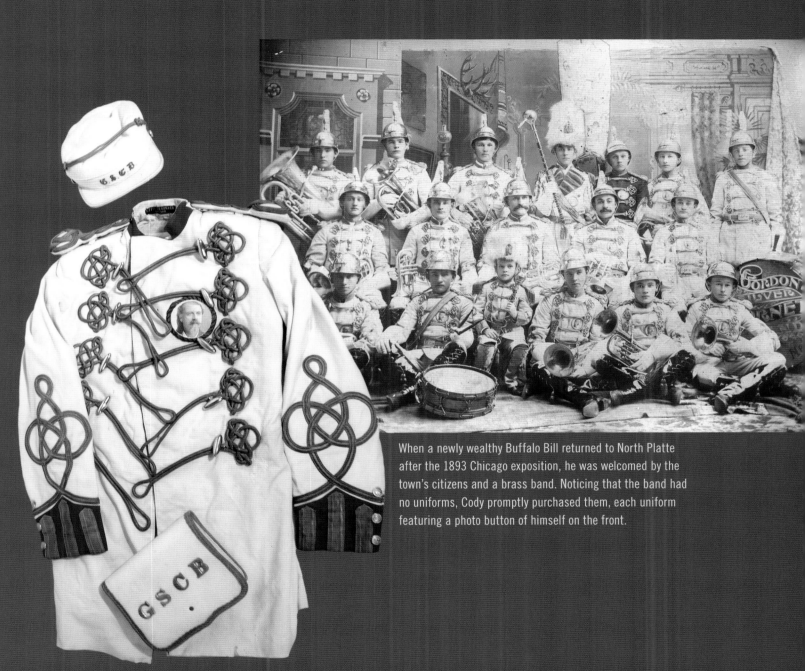

When a newly wealthy Buffalo Bill returned to North Platte after the 1893 Chicago exposition, he was welcomed by the town's citizens and a brass band. Noticing that the band had no uniforms, Cody promptly purchased them, each uniform featuring a photo button of himself on the front.

— JULY 4th 1906. —

BUFFALO BILL'S WILD WEST

SZEGED, Hungary.

Buffalo Bill's Wild West Co.

DINING DEPARTMENT.

Syracuse, N. Y. . . . July 4, 1900.

Buffalo Bill made a point of celebrating the Fourth of July with a special dinner, whether the show was at home or abroad. The *Wild West* mess tent was decorated and special menus were printed to commemorate the occasion.

The *Wild West* was a patriotic spectacle that began with the playing of "The Star-Spangled Banner" as a member of the *Wild West* rode around the arena holding the flag. This practice helped establish the song as America's national anthem. The American flag was also depicted on show outfits, including the back of Cody's jacket and these gauntlets.

Buffalo Bill invested in several Arizona mines. While they made some money, it was not enough for him to recoup his losses.

This .405-caliber Model 1895 Winchester (below) is the firearm hanging on the front of the *Wild West* gun wagon in this 1910 photograph. The label on the gun in the photograph says "Duplicate of the Gun used by Ex President Roosevelt in Africa and by Buffalo Bill in his Hunting Expeditions." The inscription on the gun reads "Presented by Col. Wm. F. Cody (Buffalo Bill)." Cody later gave it to Johnny Baker.

Product endorsements by Buffalo Bill were highly desired by companies. This advertisement for Stetson hats, always worn by Buffalo Bill, was in the *Wild West* program.

Buffalo Bill
and his
Stetson Hat

YEARS ago we made specially for Colonel Cody, the "Buffalo Bill," a soft hat of quite tremendous proportions. This style has been adopted and worn ever since by him and many of his Western companions.

Out-door life is hard on hats, and the continued patronage of these men is a strong endorsement of the satisfaction and wonderful wear that go with every "Stetson."

There are Stetson Hats for the fashionably-dressed men of the big cities, for the cowboy, the military man, the agriculturalist and every one else. Vastly different in style but highest quality always.

Soft and Stiff Felt Hats Sold by Leading Hatters Everywhere

JOHN B. STETSON COMPANY

RETAIL DEPARTMENT :
1108 Chestnut Street, Philadelphia   PHILADELPHIA

Cody continued to work on various business ideas up until his death. He patented this gun-shaped bit just before he died.

Yellowstone Park, and, of course, partnership in his show.[10]

The year before the *Wild West*'s season in Chicago, Buffalo Bill got involved in a new venture. Set in a verdant valley at the foot of Wyoming's Bighorn Mountains, the small community of Sheridan had just been reached by the Chicago, Burlington, and Quincy Railroad. Cody, who had kept an eye on that part of the country since the 1870s, formed the W. F. Cody Hotel Company and took part in a building project in the town. The Sheridan Inn became the town's largest structure and a place from which Buffalo Bill occasionally auditioned performers for the *Wild West*.[11]

Sheridan was prelude to a much greater Wyoming investment for Buffalo Bill. In 1894, he began one of his most ambitious ventures, the cofounding of a town. The following year, a plat of the new town, bearing the name of Cody City, was laid out. With its name eventually shortened to Cody, the new town would consume much of his attention and money from 1895 until his death in 1917. Although often a drain on his energy and financial resources, the town of Cody and the Bighorn Basin surrounding it became a magnet attracting Buffalo Bill back to the West more frequently than ever before. He purchased several ranches, opened the Irma Hotel (named after his daughter) in downtown Cody, and Pahaska Tepee lodge outside Yellowstone. Bearing his Lakota nickname, meaning "long hair," Pahaska Tepee was a hunting lodge that functioned as one of Buffalo Bill's favorite mountain retreats. Unfortunately, while a leading Wyoming community today, the town of Cody never quite realized Buffalo Bill's ambitions during his lifetime. Perhaps that didn't matter, because after his abortive effort to found the town of Rome, Kansas, nearly three decades earlier, he had finally founded a town, just like his father.[12]

Like Panamilt, most of Cody's investments in the New West were disappointing. He didn't live to see his plans for the town of Cody materialize. He was swindled out of much of the money he invested in his Arizona mines, which never really paid off. His Wyoming coal and water projects got bogged down in legal wrangling. Even his Yellowstone hotels were a disappointment, either losing money or only breaking even. Cody wanted to help forge the New West, but it was the *Wild West* that was his greatest success.

Emboldened by the accomplishments of the year before, Cody and his partners decided to settle *Buffalo Bill's Wild West and Congress of Rough Riders of the World* in Brooklyn's Ambrose Park for the 1894 season. Opening day drew sixteen thousand people. A newspaper reporter observed that 450 rough riders, including 135 American Indians, took part in the performance. The opening was auspicious, but audience interest was not sustainable. The show failed to bring

During the summer of 1899, Buffalo Bill arranged for his family to join Frederic Remington and his wife on a trip to Cody and one of his ranches west of town. Neither of them had been there before, and they enjoyed the trip greatly. As thanks, Remington painted one of the ranch hands and presented the portrait (right) to Buffalo Bill, who had been unable to make the trip because of the show.

After 1894, Buffalo Bill focused much of his energy on developments in and around his namesake town of Cody, Wyoming. In 1902, he opened the Irma Hotel, named after his youngest daughter. Pahaska Tepee, his hunting lodge outside Yellowstone, opened to the public in 1905. Around 1895, he purchased the TE Ranch, which he used as his primary residence when he visited Cody until he opened it as a dude ranch in 1916. These properties were aimed at providing services to tourists traveling from Cody to Yellowstone.

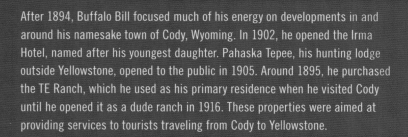

PRESENTED BY

COL. W. F. CODY (Buffalo Bill)
PRESIDENT
OF THE "BUFFALO BILL" CAVALRY SCHOOL

CODY, WYOMING

The "Buffalo Bill" Cavalry School
(In the Rockies)

A unique Military Academy, in which is taught Horsemanship, Camping, Packing, Shooting, Hunting, Military Tactics, Etc. Long trips will be taken, as a cavalry organization, through the Yellowstone National Park and adjoining mountains. ¶ The outdoor term starts June 1st, lasting five months. Only a limited number can be accommodated, so write immediately for terms and information to

MAJOR F. M. WILLIAMS,
Cody, Wyoming   N. G. Wyo., Commandant.

The Cody Military College and International Academy of Rough Riders was a short-lived project that was founded and failed in 1901, generating little more than stationery and business cards.

in the anticipated receipts over the next five months.[13]

When *Buffalo Bill's Wild West* opened again, in 1895, it did so with a new partner and a new approach. James Bailey, one of the founders of the Barnum and Bailey Circus, brought needed capital and new ideas to the show. Instead of setting up for a long run in a single city, he proposed to follow a schedule similar to that of circuses, traveling from town to town. Fifty-two train cars were acquired to transport the show.

This large nine-sheet poster promotes the Mexican vaqueros, featured performers within the *Congress of Rough Riders of the World*. Lassoing with the lariat and many other skills used by the cowboy had their origins with the vaqueros.

This new approach proved highly profitable and made Buffalo Bill an even more familiar figure throughout America's heartland. But the process required careful logistics.[14]

Several weeks before *Buffalo Bill's Wild West and Congress of Rough Riders of the World* pulled into a town, an advertising train car would arrive. In it were a group of men with advertising posters. They would canvas the town, putting up posters on the sides of barns, fences, and any other vacant surface that might provide space. In some cases, they obtained agreements from merchants to put the posters on the sides, fronts, or windows of their building in return for pay or for free passes to the show. The most common size, still used today, was a one-sheet poster measuring twenty-seven inches by forty-one inches. This paper size was sometimes patched into larger posters that were three, six, nine, and even twelve sheets in size. Sometimes an entire side of a building would be covered by a single poster. Posters for the *Wild West* were created by some of the finest lithographers of the time.

When the day of the show finally arrived, the town was already abuzz with excitement. People would even come from surrounding communities by horseback, wagon, and train to see the show and catch a glimpse of the famous Buffalo Bill. Then the trains transporting *Buffalo Bill's Wild West and Congress of Rough Riders* would pull into town.

The Courier Company of Buffalo created an advertising poster series in 1896 that depicted the various rough riders with the *Wild West*.

Advertising crews from the *Wild West* preceded the show by several weeks and would cover a town with posters. In these photos, the poster crew poses in front of the Roman Colosseum during a break from posting in the city, and posters cover a corner building in Rimini.

There would be as many as three locomotives, each pulling flat cars with show wagons, animals in livestock cars, and sleeper cars for Buffalo Bill and members of the cast.

The show would be in town for only one day, so efficiency was critical. Planks were placed on the flat cars to connect them, then each wagon was rolled to the very end and down a ramp to the ground. One wagon transported the electrical plant, which provided electricity for the large lights and spots used for nighttime performances. *Buffalo Bill's Wild West* was one of the first traveling shows to use electricity for evening performances. Another wagon was filled with ice and the food that the company would eat that day, and there were several wagons with large cook pots and stoves, critical for preparing food for a company numbering as many as six hundred persons. In many cases, the towns that hosted the show were not a whole lot larger than the show itself, which was like a small mobile city.

Once everything was off the trains, everyone lined up for the first event of the day. Indians, vaqueros, cowboys, Cossacks, buffalo, horses, and everyone else in the show paraded through the streets of the town. They were headed for the show grounds, but the parade also provided one last bit of advertising for what would be the biggest event witnessed by that town. After the tents had been unreeled and erected, the ticket wagons rolled into place, and the tepees pitched, it was time for the afternoon show. Townspeople would walk around the grounds, meeting the rough riders and the American Indians, and then finish their visit with a two-hour performance. After the performance, the staff cleaned up, ate, and prepared for an evening performance. After that, everything went in reverse order, and the show headed for the next town, repeating the whole thing the next day.

It was an exhausting schedule for Buffalo Bill and his performers. During the 1896 season, the show traveled 10,000 miles, with 132 stops. The show crossed America by rail many times over the next six years. In 1901, it played the Pan-American Exposition in Buffalo, where Cody met Calamity Jane and Geronimo. Even though their names have been occasionally linked with his, neither became a performer in his *Wild West*. Not long after that, a major train

Vouchers were used to pay poster crews for their services. These unused vouchers were produced for the tours of Italy and Germany in 1906.

wreck killed many of the animals and injured Annie Oakley. During her recuperation, she decided to leave the *Wild West*, having toured with it for nearly sixteen years.[15]

Following the 1901 season, Cody, James Bailey, and Nate Salsbury hatched a plan to return to Europe. The Barnum and Bailey Circus would soon finish a tour there and was to return to America. The *Wild West* could go to Europe and use the circus's rolling stock (wagons, train car, etc.). The circus could do the same in America, thus saving expenses for each show. With the two major shows on different continents, they would also not compete with each other.

In December of 1902, *Buffalo Bill's Wild West* returned to Europe, beginning the tour in England. Now it included the *Congress of Rough Riders of the World* as well as sideshows, one of Bailey's innovations. The sideshows included such curiosities as a moss-haired lady, a blue man, and a snake charmer. Despite protestations by publicist John Burke, the *Wild West* was becoming more of a show and less of an educational exhibition. By this time, people in the United States had grown used to and a little bit tired of the *Wild West*. The people of Europe, on the other hand, had not seen the show for a decade. Record crowds attended the show as it toured England, Scotland, France, Belgium, Italy, and the Austro-Hungarian Empire.

But there were incidents during the European tour that cast a pall over the elation that Cody might otherwise have felt. On December 24, 1902, just two days before the show opened in London, Nate Salsbury died. The loss of Salsbury, who had been ill for some time, was a terrible loss for the *Wild West*. From the beginning, Salsbury, Cody, and Burke had formed a winning team, founding the *Wild West* and propelling it to success. After that, in 1906, James Bailey died, and his estate insisted upon repayment of his interest in the show. The incident that really shook Cody, however, was much more personal. In January 30, 1904, his oldest daughter, Arta, who had accompanied him on his first tour of Europe, passed away.[16]

By the time of Arta's death, the tensions between Buffalo Bill and Louisa had escalated. In 1902 he had written his sister Julia, "Some of the very best people in the world are getting divorced every day. They say it's better than going on living a life of misery for both." He said he wanted a quiet legal separation and that Louisa would receive a nice financial settlement. He was concerned, however, about Arta's reaction. While he didn't file for divorce at the time, the talk of divorce continued. Then, after Arta's death, Louisa accused Buffalo Bill of breaking their daughter's heart. After nearly thirty years of fighting, it was the last straw, and within two weeks Will Cody filed for divorce.[17]

This illustration on the back of a *Wild West* souvenir shows the layout of the *Wild West*, with the central arena, Indian village, mess tent, and wheeled electric generators.

One of the *Wild West*'s American Indian policemen poses with a friend in Manchester, England, in 1903.

Large, portable electric generators provided lighting in the show's tents and arena. The *Wild West* was one of the first outdoor shows to use electricity for its nighttime shows.

This billy club belonged to a member of the *Wild West*'s American Indian police. Order was maintained in the *Wild West*, which eventually swelled to over six hundred staff and cast members, by giving select individuals authority to enforce show rules. These included Indian police, who monitored the behavior of the tribal members of the show.

This advance courier (below) was used to promote appearances by the *Wild West* in 1898 and 1899.

1899 *Wild West* program.

1895 *Wild West* program.

This signed ticket (right) for complimentary admission was given by Cody to William House, a performer with the *Wild West*, for distribution to a family member or friend.

After the *Wild West*'s successful season in Chicago, it relocated to Ambrose Park in Brooklyn for five months in the summer of 1894. The following year the show went back on the road, traveling America until the fall of 1902.

This unsigned and unused complimentary admission ticket to the *Wild West* was issued in 1902.

During the *Wild West*'s tour of England from 1902 to 1904, Johnny Baker served as arenic director, overseeing the activities in the *Wild West*'s show arena. Baker's photo album from the tour offers unique behind-the-scenes glimpses of the show's operations, including the performers relaxing together.

Buffalo Bill's Wild West and Congress of Rough Riders of the World returned to Europe in late 1902 after nearly ten years' absence. It included new acts, like a demonstration of lifesaving at sea, as well as sideshows.

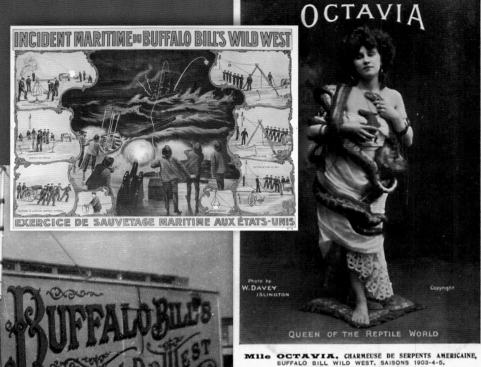

A program, a booklet showing the show's route, and an admission ticket, all from the *Wild West*'s tour of the United Kingdom from 1902 through 1904. Signed by Jule Keen, treasurer for the *Wild West*, the ticket was used for admission to the show in Walsall, England, on April 27, 1904.

Chapter Seven
Friends, Family, and Faith
1905–1912

*I believe that a man gets closer to God out there in the big, free West…You feel differently about your fellow man out there in the West. He's nearer to you and God is nearer to you. You are filled with a true religion and a bigger realization of life. **Buffalo Bill, 1907***

After years of conflict and a separation of nearly a decade, Will and Louisa Cody finally reunited in 1911. In this photo, taken after their reconciliation, Buffalo Bill demonstrates genuine affection for his wife.

It had been a bad year. Buffalo Bill had hoped that Louisa would take the money he offered and let the marriage quietly dissolve. He had stayed with her for the children as much as anything. But now Irma was married and Arta had died so unexpectedly from meningitis. Still, Louisa had fought the divorce. The trial had been awful, with their family's problems plastered on the front pages of newspapers across the country, and even in Europe. And then the judge had chided him and refused his divorce request. That too had been front-page news. Alone in his hotel room, Buffalo Bill felt more discouraged than he had in a long time.

The failed divorce attempt, the deaths of his daughter Arta and longtime business partner Salsbury, financial disappointments, and personal health problems weighed heavily on Will Cody as he began the 1905 season in France. He was beaten down, both psychologically and physically. As low as he had ever been in his life, he turned to family, friends, and God.

Buffalo Bill had always supported his sisters, buying them houses and investing in their husbands' businesses after he became a financial success. He was closest to his eldest sister, Julia, with whom he corresponded frequently and to whom he revealed his deepest thoughts. A devout Christian, Julia was concerned about the state of her brother's soul and told him so in a letter in 1901. He had put her off at the time. He had not been particularly religious in his life, and after the disastrous stand years earlier in New Orleans had even thought he might become an atheist. But in spring of 1905, he had a change of heart. He wrote Julia: "And it's in my old age I have found God—And realize how easy it is to abandon sin and serve him. When one stops to think how little they have to give up—to serve God. It's a wonder so many don't do it. A person only has to do right."[1]

The date Buffalo Bill wrote the letter to Julia, June 14, 1905, marked a change in Cody. Not only did he continue to write about his faith in letters to his family and close associates, he stopped drinking and rarely, if ever, touched alcohol for the rest of his life. He was fairly private about his beliefs but did share them occasionally. After a show for the inmates at New York's Auburn Prison, he admonished them to put their faith in God. He even made some changes in the show, writing to Julia, "No swearing or drinking in my Company since I got good." This turn to God and the desire to do right may also

have been the beginning of Buffalo Bill's return to his wife, Louisa.[2]

The Codys' divorce trial, held in Cheyenne, Wyoming, had made all of the private angers and accusations very public. Buffalo Bill accused Louisa of trying to poison him, while she accused him of carrying on with other women. A parade of friends and family servants filed onto the witness stand, testifying on behalf of one or the other. Finally, the judge ruled against Buffalo Bill's petition for divorce on March 23, 1905, stating that Cody had responded to Louisa's wifely devotion with cruelty and had "heaped indignities upon her." Shortly after the ruling, *Buffalo Bill's Wild West and Congress of Rough Riders of the World* left for Paris, where it appeared for two months on the Champs de Mars. The tour of Europe continued for the next two years, allowing the Codys time apart after the acrimonious trial.[3]

In 1907, the *Wild West* returned from Europe and began touring the United States. Even though on the same continent, the two Codys remained apart. When not on tour, Buffalo Bill avoided North Platte, spending most of his time in Wyoming. But their relationship had always been filled with affection as well as enmity. During the next three years, they each struggled with these conflicting feelings while the wounds from the divorce trial slowly healed. In the meantime, their remaining daughter, Irma, and Arta's son, Cody Boal, turned their attention

Fifteen years after the show's first visit, *Buffalo Bill's Wild West* returned to Paris for a two-month stand. The show was located to the heart of the city, on the Champs de Mars, in front of the Eiffel Tower. In the background is a Ferris wheel, erected for an exposition in 1900 and still in use in 1905.

This photograph of Buffalo Bill, taken around 1905, was his foster son Johnny Baker's favorite. The photograph was the inspiration for a poster used to promote the *Wild West* during its stay in Paris.

117

HERE WE ARE!
HOME AGAIN FROM FOREIGN LANDS.

Buffalo Bill's Wild West played to enthusiastic audiences for four seasons in Europe. The show then began its 1907 American tour with a two-month stand at New York's Madison Square Garden, one of Buffalo Bill's favorite venues.

A *Wild West* program from the 1907 season.

This advance courier was distributed to promote the *Wild West* in 1907 and 1908.

A complimentary ticket for a September 28, 1908, appearance in Medford, Oregon.

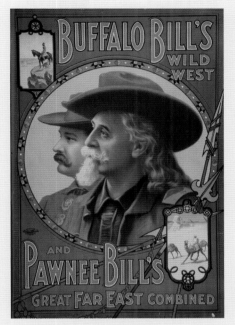

In 1909, Buffalo Bill combined his show with that of his competitor Pawnee Bill. The combined show continued to promote the West, offering new acts such as cowboys and American Indians competing on horseback in a game of football. It also included exotic acts from foreign lands.

to reuniting the couple. They invited Buffalo Bill to return to North Platte for Easter of 1910. When he arrived, they took him to Scout's Rest Ranch, where Louisa was waiting. Neither was expecting to see the other. Left alone in a room, the couple reconciled, resolving to spend their remaining years together. Over the next seven years, the affection they had always held for each other blossomed, and finally there was little quarreling in the household.[4]

While Buffalo Bill was struggling with his feelings about Louisa, he also came to terms with an old acquaintance turned competitor. Gordon Lillie had worked for Buffalo Bill during the first season of the *Wild West*, in 1882, appearing in the show and also onstage. This helped launch his own show business career as Pawnee Bill, and by 1907 he was one of Cody's fiercest competitors. But after twenty-five years of *Wild West* shows, Americans were looking for something newer and more exotic than the vanished Old West. Cody's rough riders now included Japanese horsemen and Hawaiian cowboys. Cody also incorporated a re-creation of the Battle of Peking in the show. Lillie had already changed his show title to *Pawnee Bill's Historic Far West and Great Far East*, integrating trained elephants and acts from India. Since gate receipts were still down for both companies, Cody and Lillie realized that there might be an advantage to combining forces. They

119

A cast photo of *Buffalo Bill's Wild West and Pawnee Bill's Far East* taken in 1910.

The first program (above) issued by Buffalo Bill and Pawnee Bill after they combined forces in 1909. Their combined show toured the United States for the next four years.

Buffalo Bill and Pawnee Bill, usually pictured in buckskin, looking like two ordinary businessmen in 1910 (above).

After the 1909 merger, Buffalo Bill and his new partner vigorously promoted the skills of the show's cowgirls, which included bronco riders Lulu Parr and Goldie Griffith, as well as Pawnee Bill's wife, May Lillie.

Goldie Griffith.

Lulu Parr.

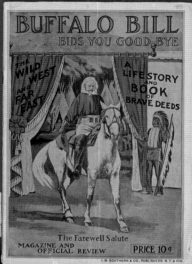

After a successful season with Pawnee Bill in 1909, Buffalo Bill decided he would finally retire. The partners launched a two-year program of farewell tours that were financially successful. Unfortunately, bad investments prevented Cody from retiring as planned once the tours concluded. These are the farewell programs from 1910 and 1911.

"Buffalo Bill's Farewell March and Two Step" sheet music, published and distributed in the United States and Europe in 1910 and 1911.

Edison Amberol's four-minute recording of "Buffalo Bill's Farewell March and Two Step," as performed by the New York Military Band.

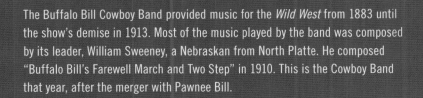

The Buffalo Bill Cowboy Band provided music for the *Wild West* from 1883 until the show's demise in 1913. Most of the music played by the band was composed by its leader, William Sweeney, a Nebraskan from North Platte. He composed "Buffalo Bill's Farewell March and Two Step" in 1910. This is the Cowboy Band that year, after the merger with Pawnee Bill.

121

arrived upon the title *Buffalo Bill's Wild West and Pawnee Bill's Far East*, and began 1909 as a combined show.[5]

In 1910, a sixty-four-year-old Buffalo Bill, perhaps motivated in part by his reconciliation with Louisa, decided it was finally time to retire. He had been talking about retirement for many years, but this time he decided to make it formal. Cody announced his impending retirement at Madison Square Garden in May and embarked on two years of farewell tours with Lillie.

Buffalo Bill and Pawnee Bill announced a series of farewell performances in 1910. Over the next two years, their combined show crossed America several times as Buffalo Bill said good-bye to his fans.

At the outset, the farewell tours proved successful, as public sentiment drove visitors to the show to see Buffalo Bill for the last time. Nineteen hundred ten was a good year, but poor weather near the end of 1911 cramped the partners' profits. Cody continued to pour his portion of the show profits into his other business interests, including his Oracle mine in Arizona and his efforts to develop the Bighorn Valley around Cody. When the farewell tours concluded, he discovered he could not afford to retire. So the partners quietly dropped any mention of farewell tours from their publicity and continued the show in 1912.

As Buffalo Bill aged, he was surrounded and supported by men who owed their success to him. Foremost among them was Johnny Baker, who had met Cody as a nine-year-old in 1878 and joined the Wild West in 1883. Baker grew up with the *Wild West*, learning to become an expert marksman from Cody and other performers in the show. Within the decade, he was providing exhibition shooting as "The Cowboy Kid," and by 1893 he was a headliner. After the deaths of first Nate Salsbury and then James Bailey, Baker assumed more and more responsibility for the management of the show, in addition to performing. During the extended tour of Europe from 1902 to 1907, his official title was arenic manager. After the merger with Pawnee Bill, Baker continued in his management role.

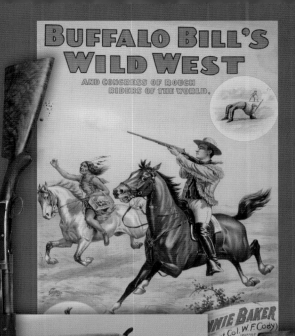

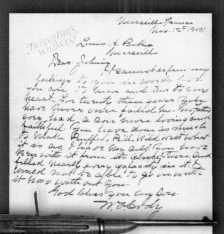

This Winchester Model 1895 carbine was presented by Johnny Baker to Buffalo Bill on the occasion of his sixtieth birthday. The inscription reads: "To my Governor, Col. W. F. Cody from Johnny Baker, 1906."

Buffalo Bill's foster son, Johnny Baker, was one of the most important members of the *Wild West*, acting as show manager in addition to demonstrating marksmanship skills.

Marseille France
Nov. 12th 1908

Dear Johnie,

I cannot express my feelings to you in words for you are so near and dear to my heart. For twenty-three years you have never once failed me. No Father ever had a son more loving and faithful. You have done as much to make Buffalo Bills Wild West what it is as I have myself. You have been with it from its conception and filled nearly every capacity in it. I would not be able to go on with it now without you.

God bless you my Son,

W. F. Cody

This bench was carved in Brienz, Switzerland, and was probably purchased by Johnny Baker as a gift for Buffalo Bill during the 1906 tour of Italy.

In an expression of affection and gratitude, Cody wrote to Baker, "No father ever had a son more loving and faithful. You have done as much to make the *Wild West* what it is as I have myself."[6]

There were others, as well. Buffalo Bill's faithful publicist, John Burke, who had been with him since the Combination days, continued to handle public relations for the combined *Buffalo Bill's Wild West and Pawnee Bill's Far East*. In this role he was assisted by newcomer Frank Winch. Winch, who also grew close to Cody, wrote *Thrilling Lives of Buffalo Bill and Pawnee Bill*, which sold as a show souvenir for $1.00.

Another friend to whom Cody turned during this time was Lakota chief Iron Tail. Iron Tail had been at the Battle of Little Bighorn. Later he was wounded and most of his family killed at Wounded Knee. He joined *Buffalo Bill's Wild West* and was eventually put in charge of the American Indian performers. The friendship between the two grew as Iron Tail accompanied Cody on hunting and business trips. He is often seen in photographs with Buffalo Bill and his other friends. In 1901, it was Iron Tail who suggested that Cody's new lodge outside Yellowstone be called Pahaska, Buffalo Bill's Lakota nickname. Cody later reciprocated by naming one of his Arizona mining claims after Iron Tail.[7]

As a young man, Buffalo Bill had learned the importance of organizational affiliations. He was one of the charter members of the North Platte Masonic Lodge when it was founded in 1869 and continued his association with the Masons throughout his life. During the 1887 to 1888 tour of England, he was welcomed with open arms by his fellow Masons, who invited him to a number of special dinners and events. In 1894, he became a 32 Degree Mason of the New York City Consistory. As a Master Mason, Buffalo Bill also became a lifetime member of the Shriners' Tangier Temple in Omaha. Buffalo Bill's path back to North Platte frequently included stops in Omaha. He joined the Omaha Elks Lodge in 1897 and remained a member throughout the rest of his life. Both the Elks and the Masons later filled prominent roles at his funeral and burial.

Buffalo Bill's affiliation with the Masons was nearly terminated in 1905. The adverse publicity given his divorce trial led the North Platte lodge to consider ejecting him from the ranks of the Masons. Since Cody was in France at the time and not able to defend himself from the charges, his sister Julia prevailed upon the Masons to keep him as a member.[8]

Prior to his departure to Britain in 1887, Buffalo Bill had been appointed aide-de-camp in the Nebraska National Guard, receiving the rank of colonel. This had been primarily a business move, since it was felt that the title of colonel would give him added credibility with the Europeans. This appointment proved to be useful to the National

Iron Tail, Johnny Baker, James Bailey, Buffalo Bill (all seated, left to right), and various family members pose around the dinner table, circa 1900.

Iron Tail's headdress, worn by him in this photograph taken with Buffalo Bill around 1906.

Iron Tail was one of three American Indians who modeled for the Indian image on the Buffalo nickel.

Guard as well. In 1889, Governor Thayer gave Cody the rank of general and later asked him to assist with the Indian problems associated with the Ghost Dance. The presence of such a well-known personage as a member of the Nebraska National Guard also added to its prestige and to that of Governor Thayer. This desire to associate with Buffalo Bill was repeated in Wyoming, when in 1907 the governor appointed him as his aide-de-camp with a rank of major in the Wyoming National Guard.

Cody's memberships and appointments were vital to his business interests. They were mentioned in publicity for the *Wild West*, and he traded on the connections they gave him as he pursued his real estate and mining interests.

There was one group of friends that did not provide Buffalo Bill with any vital business connections and that demanded little from him. Yet he had as deep an affection for them as for any group with which he was affiliated: his horses. He had loved horses since he was a boy and included horsemanship as a central aspect of his *Wild West*. Even after he paired with *Pawnee Bill's Far East*, with the addition of more exotic beasts like elephants and camels, Buffalo Bill insisted that feats of horsemanship be central to the show.

Over his lifetime, Buffalo Bill regularly rode more than twenty different horses, ranging from his old hunting buddy Brigham to Isham, his last show horse. While traveling through France in 1905, the *Wild West* was struck by tragedy. An outbreak of glanders, a disease deadly to horses and potentially harmful to humans, led to the death or euthanization of two hundred horses that were part of the show. Among them was Cody's horse Prince, named after the pony presented to him by his father when he was a child.[9]

Buffalo Bill's love of the outdoors increasingly drew him back to his TE Ranch outside Cody, Wyoming. It was here that he hoped to retire after his series of farewell shows.

Commemorative *Buffalo Bill's Wild West and Pawnee Bill's Far East* watch fob, inscribed to the Shriners' Mecca Temple while the show was in New York City in 1909.

Buffalo Bill became a member of the North Platte chapter of Masons in 1870. This is a receipt for Cody's dues to the North Platte chapter of Masons in 1894.

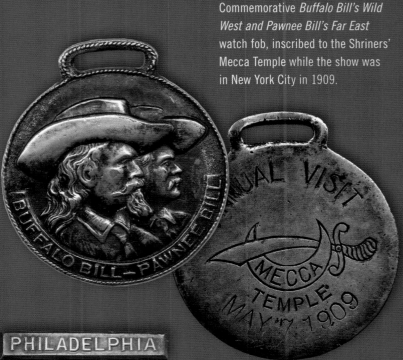

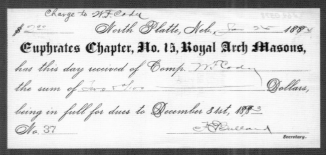

PHILADELPHIA

Medal awarded to Buffalo Bill from the Shriners' Lu Lu Temple in Philadelphia, 1912.

In 1894, Buffalo Bill became a member of the Scottish Rite of Freemasonry and, in one day, moved from a 4 Degree to 32 Degree. Even though his schedule kept him from being an active member, this rapid ascent in degrees recognized Buffalo Bill's larger contribution to the values espoused by the Masons. This is the 32 Degree Mason certificate and medal that he received from the Consistory of New York City in 1894.

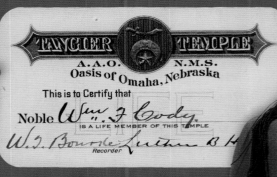

As Cody moved up the ranks within the Masons, he also became a Shriner, joining the Tangier Shrine Temple in Omaha, 1892. He received this fez and lifetime membership card from the Tangier Shrine Temple at that time.

Nebraska's Governor Thayer appointed Buffalo Bill to the rank of colonel in the National Guard in 1887, just before the *Wild West* departed for England. Even though he was later appointed to other ranks in both the Nebraska and Wyoming National Guards, Cody preferred the title of colonel. In 1892, he was presented with this sword and scabbard by the Nebraska National Guard.

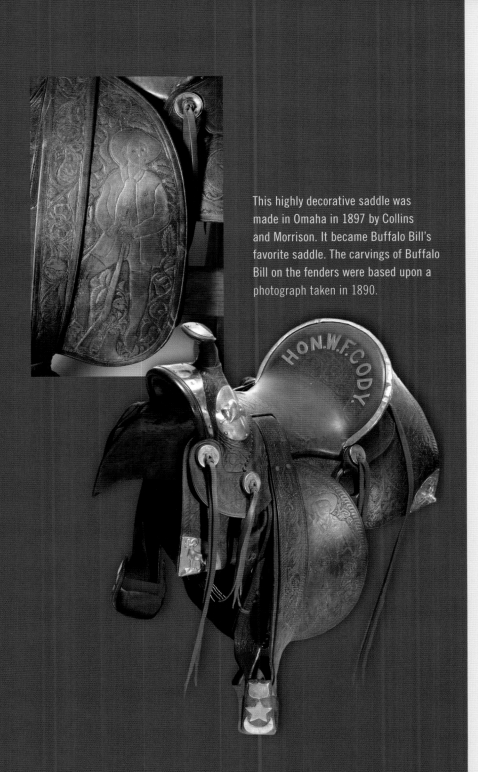

This highly decorative saddle was made in Omaha in 1897 by Collins and Morrison. It became Buffalo Bill's favorite saddle. The carvings of Buffalo Bill on the fenders were based upon a photograph taken in 1890.

The stage scenery of the *Wild West* may have been the most realistic depiction of the West seen by show audiences, but Buffalo Bill knew that the real thing was much more. From 1886 through 1905, Buffalo Bill had made every effort he could to get back to the West, participating in hunting expeditions, visiting North Platte, and assisting with the Ghost Dance situation. But he hadn't been able to spend the extended times there that he really enjoyed. And there were some years when he didn't get to the West at all. Fortunately, taking care of business in the town of Cody and at his various resorts near Yellowstone afforded him some time in his favorite part of the world. As Buffalo Bill neared retirement, his thoughts turned more and more to the West. As he told the crowd during his first farewell speech at Madison Square Garden in 1910, "I am about to go home for a well-earned rest." But it was not to be.[10]

Muson was one of several pure-blood Arabian horses imported by Homer Davenport in 1906. Davenport presented Muson to Buffalo Bill to ride during the *Wild West*'s two-month appearance at Madison Square Garden in 1907, after the show's return from Europe. Here Muson wears Cody's favorite saddle (left).

Duke was presented to Buffalo Bill by General Nelson Miles in the 1890s. Here Cody rides Duke using his favorite Collins and Morrison saddle (right). When Duke died, one of his leg bones was carved into the image of a buffalo and given to Cody for use as an umbrella handle (below).

This paperweight was made from a silver horse-shoe from Duke and a hoof from Prince. While the *Wild West* was touring France, a disease broke out among the horses, killing nearly two hundred. The inscription on the hoof reads: "To Colonel Cody, Souvenir of his faithful servant Prince, Who died at Marseilles, France, Dec. 6, 1905."

130

Chapter Eight
The Final Stands

1913–1917

The show business isn't what it used to be. *Buffalo Bill, 1913*

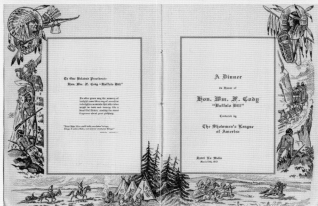

Buffalo Bill returned to his seat after delivering his thanks. As much as he appreciated the honor accorded him by the Showman's League, he really hoped this presidency would be his final act in show business. Too many dinners, too many speeches, and too many miles. He longed to return to the West, settle down on his ranch, and enjoy that well-deserved rest he had told everyone he was going to take. But the 1912 season had not brought in the anticipated receipts, and his other businesses were struggling. Maybe the 1913 season would be more successful. The loan he got from Harry Tammen should help a lot.

In 1913, Buffalo Bill became the first president of the newly formed Showman's League of America. This came despite the fact that the public's interest in *Wild West* shows had waned and Cody had been saying for years that he wanted to

Buffalo Bill helped found the Showman's League of America. The following year, the group held a special dinner recognizing him as their president.

retire from show business. The farewell tours from 1910 to 1912 had been intended to herald that retirement, but Buffalo Bill and his partner, Pawnee Bill, did not make as much money as they had intended. And Cody's other investments were doing very poorly. So, even though audience numbers had diminished, Buffalo Bill kept at it.

In January of 1913, Cody made what seemed like a shrewd business move at the time, but which turned out to be a disaster. He had known Denver's Harry Tammen for some time. Tammen was an extraordinary, if not always honest, entrepreneur. And he was interested in making a loan to help finance the next season for *Buffalo Bill's Wild West and Pawnee Bill's Far East*. His six-month loan of $20,000 would pay for some of

the expenses involved in getting the show on the road. Buffalo Bill anticipated that he would be able to pay the loan back by the time it was due.[1]

What Buffalo Bill did not realize was that Tammen wanted him to become a part of Tammen's own show, the Sells-Floto Circus. After the loan agreement was made, Tammen announced that in 1914 *Buffalo Bill's Wild West* would separate from *Pawnee Bill's Far East* and become associated with Sells-Floto. Cody's partner, Pawnee Bill, was infuriated. Cody told him that no such agreement existed, but the damage was already done, so the 1913 season started on a sour note. Things didn't get any better. Bad weather and other problems plagued the show after it opened in April. By the

On January 21, 1913, William Cody telegraphed his partner, G. W. Lillie (Pawnee Bill), in Pawnee, Oklahoma, asking for authorization to get a loan from Harry Tammen of Denver. Lillie presented a handwritten reply to be telegraphed to Cody in North Platte authorizing him to "make loan and sign same for *Buffalo Bill's Wild West and Pawnee Bills Far East*."

The last program for *Buffalo Bill's Wild West*, now combined with *Pawnee Bill's Far East*, was used in 1912 and during the final season of 1913.

Buffalo Bill wrote, "For twenty-eight years I have hammered one spot daily until the spot has grown too sore to stand it any longer." By 1912, Cody was spending less time in the saddle and more time riding in carriages, even during the show. He wore formal dress while in his carriage, a phaeton drawn by two horses, reserving the wearing of buckskins for when he was in the saddle.

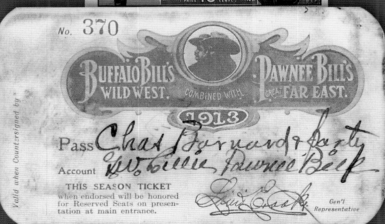

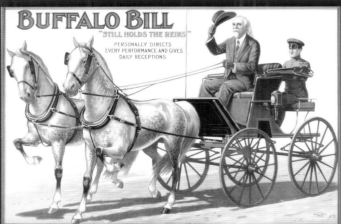

This season pass became useless after the combined *Buffalo Bill's Wild West and Pawnee Bill's Far East* was closed and auctioned off in Denver in August of 1913.

These were part of Buffalo Bill's last show outfit, pictured in a photograph taken around 1915 and later depicted in a series of paintings by Robert Lindneux. The hat was worn by him at his last public appearance, on November 11, 1916.

When the *Wild West* was sold at auction in 1913, Buffalo Bill almost lost his favorite horse, Isham. The saddle worn by Isham in this photo was made for Buffalo Bill in 1897 by Collins and Morrison of Omaha.

time the show reached Denver for performances on July 21 and 22, the note to Tammen was due and the partners were in debt to other lenders as well.[2]

At the conclusion of the July 21 performance, the Denver sheriff descended on the show. Tammen had succeeded in persuading the other creditors to join him in seizing the show and closing it down. After a month of court proceedings, *Buffalo Bill's Wild West and Pawnee Bill's Far East* went on the auction block at Denver's Overland Park. The sale took several days. After the final day, a reporter observed, "The bidding was fast. To the man who doesn't know what a thousand dollars looks like, it seemed that the men out there cared no more for a hundred dollar bill than a hog does for Sunday."[3]

Included in the assets sold on August 21 was Buffalo Bill's favorite horse, Isham. Cody had acquired Isham after his warhorse Charley died at sea while returning from England in 1888. Even though over the years Buffalo Bill was both painted and photographed riding Tucker, Duke, Muson, Prince, and other horses, he had a special connection with Isham. The two of them had grown old together, and Cody commented that "we know each other better than brothers." Present on the day of the auction were close friends and acquaintances who engaged in spirited bidding for Isham. When Isham was purchased for $150 by Cody's old friend Colonel C. J. Bills of

Nebraska, it became clear that he and the others had bid on Isham for the sole purpose of presenting him to Buffalo Bill. Man and horse were reunited as onlookers cried tears of joy.[4]

By the end of August, Tammen had achieved his objective. Buffalo Bill's partnership with Pawnee Bill was dissolved, *Buffalo Bill's Wild West* was dispersed, and Buffalo Bill would now have to appear with the Sells-Floto Circus during its 1914 season. Cody would later write, "H. H. Tammen was the man who had my show sold at sheriff sale which broke my heart." But Cody was also pragmatic enough to realize he was going to have to work things out with Tammen if he was ever going to have his own show again. And he had an idea.[5]

William F. Cody had always kept an eye on the future. During his days onstage, he had anticipated the popularity of large outdoor shows. He was fascinated with the new technologies of his time and was one of the first to use outdoor electric lighting for evening performances. He knew and admired Thomas Edison, whom he considered the greatest genius of his time. In the 1890s, Thomas Edison had filmed the *Wild West* using his newly invented Kinetoscope. By 1913, the new media of moving pictures had become popular, beginning with *The Great Train Robbery* in 1903 and continuing with Broncho Billy Anderson's many movies. In 1912, Buffalo Bill and Pawnee Bill formed the

Buffalo Bill/Pawnee Bill Film Company. Their *Life of Buffalo Bill*, released by Barnsdales' Moving Pictures and promoted by a series of posters, experienced moderate success. That success was, however, overshadowed by the larger problems they were having with their other investments, particularly their show.

Cody's idea was to create a series of historical moving pictures, starting with a film about the Indian Wars. Despite his unfortunate experience with Tammen, Cody approached him and his business partner, Frederick Bonfils, with the idea. They liked it. In fall of 1913, with the backing of Tammen and Bonfils, Buffalo Bill launched The Col. W. F. Cody (Buffalo Bill) Historical Pictures Co. Broncho Billy Anderson's Essanay Films would do the filming and Johnny Baker would be the director. This ambitious project needed the cooperation of the US Army, which Cody was able to obtain through his friendship with General Nelson Miles. Permission to engage American Indians from the Pine Ridge Reservation in the endeavor was obtained from the Department of the Interior. Many of the retired US Army soldiers and American Indians who had roles in the movie had been present at the actual battles being reenacted. The most poignant, and most dangerous, part of the filming occurred at Wounded Knee. Lakota men and women who either had been at Wounded Knee or had family

Life of Buffalo Bill

ACTUAL MOVING PICTURES by CODY, HIMSELF.

Thrilling Adventures of the Famous Scout and Indian Fighter, Colonel W. F. Cody.

500 Indians on the War Path.... Famous Battle Scenes as they actually occurred.

The famous old Sante Fe Trail, and Life on the Plains as it used to be.

More Cowboys, Scouts, Soldiers and Indians than ever appeared in any other production.

PRICES—In nearly all cities you can see in the picture houses moving pictures forty minutes, about ten minutes of advertising slides, and ten more to rewind and adjust the reels; this is called a one hour show, and costs ten cents. Our actual exhibition time is over two hours, we show more film each night than the city shows use in a week. WE GUARANTEE MORE FOR THE MONEY THAN YOU CAN GET ELSEWHERE.

Created in 1912, *Life of Buffalo Bill* was Cody's first effort to capture the excitement of the West using the new media of film.

Cody's second film, made in 1913, was a documentary about the Indian Wars, filmed at Wounded Knee and other battle sites. It included a scene of Buffalo Bill taking the "first scalp for Custer." This beaded belt was worn by Cody during the movie.

137

killed there participated in the filming but were very upset. Some of the young warriors even talked about taking vengeance on the soldiers who had killed their friends and family. When older members of the Lakota found out about the plan, they intervened, and the filming was done without bloodshed.[6]

Buffalo Bill may have hoped that his epic film would make enough money for him to bankroll a new show. It didn't. The public showed little interest in the film, and eventually it disappeared. Today, while the *Life of Buffalo Bill* movie is mostly intact, all that remains of *The Indian Wars* are a few film fragments and still photographs taken during the filming.

After a winter spent promoting the new movie, Buffalo Bill joined the cast of the Sells-Floto Circus, now publicized as including the "Original *Buffalo Bill's Wild West*." But about all that remained of the *Wild West* was Buffalo Bill. Johnny Baker, who continued to assist Cody with his other business efforts, had nothing to do with the show and went to Europe to take part in shooting exhibitions. Sells-Floto was a circus, and a third-rate one at that, with one class act, and that was Buffalo Bill. After the 1914 season concluded, Cody reluctantly signed on for the 1915 season, still hoping to make enough money to start his own show.[7]

By the conclusion of the 1915 season, Buffalo Bill had had enough of Sells-Floto and of Tammen. He wrote a friend, "This man is driving me crazy. I can easily kill him but as I avoided killing in the bad days I don't want to kill him." In September, he and Tammen had a showdown, with Cody coming dangerously close to breaking that resolve. Cody finally quit, swearing, "I'll never go out with this show again."[8]

Buffalo Bill endured his two years with the Sells-Floto Circus with the hope that he would be able to accumulate enough capital to bring back his *Wild West*. During those difficult years, he sat at the portable desk in his tent, outlining ideas for a new show and writing friends for support. But when Cody finally left Sells-Floto, he was reminded by Tammen that he could not use the name *Buffalo Bill's Wild West*. In fact, to even use his own name in another show, he would need to pay Tammen $5,000.[9]

Finally free of Tammen, Cody spent the winter of 1915 to 1916 lecturing with his films and working on a new autobiography, which was serialized by *Hearst's International* magazine. He paid off Tammen for use of his name and began appearing with the Miller and Arlington Wild West Show Company that spring. By this time their show, associated with the Miller Brothers' 101 Ranch in Oklahoma, was one of the last western shows still touring. Unable to raise enough money to do his own show, Cody was able to persuade them to stage one of his ideas. "The Military Pageant of Preparedness" would play to the public's concern about the war in Europe.

This painting of Buffalo Bill was created by the United States Lithograph Company for use as a poster. The back of the painting has directions for poster production, including the addition of Buffalo Bill's signature and quantities to be printed. At least two different posters were created using the painting.

This complimentary ticket (left) was authorized by John Burke, one of Buffalo Bill's only friends able to accompany him during the troubled two seasons with the Sells-Floto Circus.

Even though Harry Tammen forced *Buffalo Bill's Wild West and Pawnee Bill's Far East* out of business, his Sells-Floto Circus altered and sold souvenir card decks that had been associated with their show.

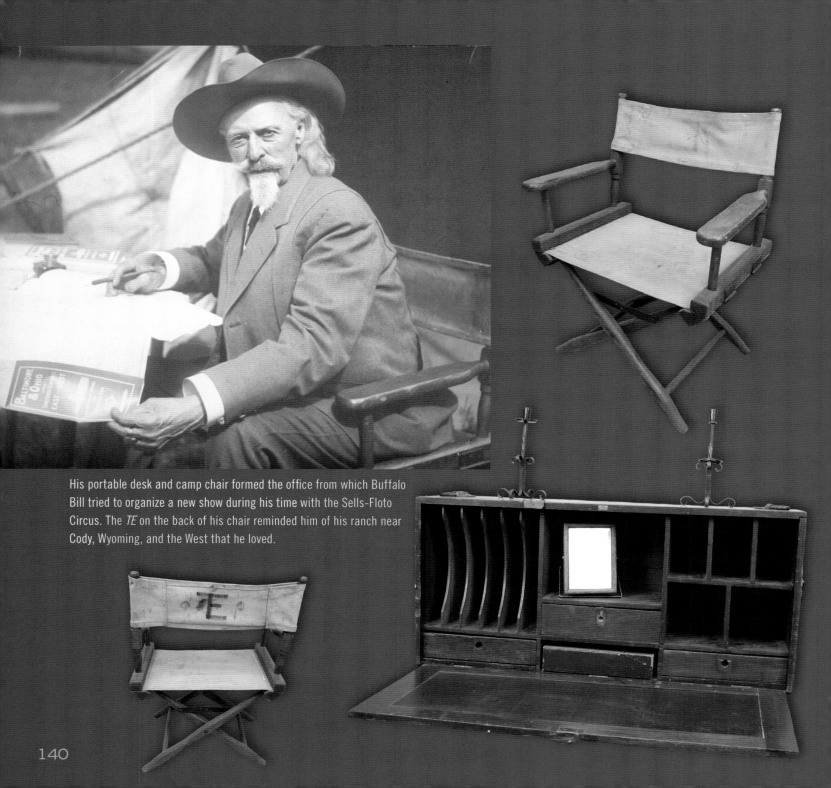

His portable desk and camp chair formed the office from which Buffalo Bill tried to organize a new show during his time with the Sells-Floto Circus. The *TE* on the back of his chair reminded him of his ranch near Cody, Wyoming, and the West that he loved.

Batteries of field guns and cavalry exercises reflected the preparedness theme, but much of the program still included elements of Cody's old *Wild West* show. Since Cody could use his own name but not the full *Buffalo Bill's Wild West* name, the show was billed as featuring "Buffalo Bill (himself)."[10]

Buffalo Bill's brief time with the *101 Ranch Wild West* show was happy. It was not a circus but a real western show,

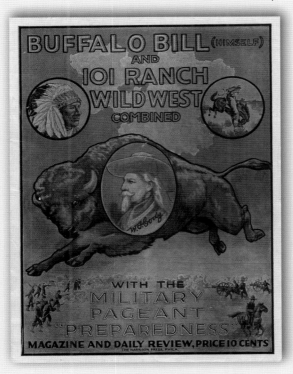

After severing his arrangement with Harry Tammen to appear with the Sells-Floto Circus, Buffalo Bill joined the *101 Ranch Wild West*. He spent one season with them before his death.

with cowboys and cowgirls, vaqueros and Indians. And he was reunited with his old friends Johnny Baker and Iron Tail. Unfortunately, Iron Tail developed pneumonia and died in May. Cody himself, at age seventy, could barely sit on a horse and often rode through the arena in a carriage. When he did ride, he needed Baker's assistance getting in and out of the saddle. When the 1916 season ended in November, he headed to Denver for a visit with his sister May and then continued on to his TE Ranch outside Cody, Wyoming.[11]

By the end of 1916, when he returned to Denver to spend more time with his sister, Buffalo Bill was gravely ill. In hopes of aiding a recovery, he took the train to Glenwood Springs to take in the waters. There he was told that he had little time left and should return to Denver to wrap up his affairs. When he arrived at his sister's house in Denver in early January, the word went out across the nation: the great scout was at death's door.

Buffalo Bill's last days were consumed with tying up loose ends. He granted his last interview to Chauncey Thomas, a friend and writer for *Outdoor Life*, played cards with some friends, and waited for his remaining family members to join him. On January 9, he asked to be baptized by Father Christopher Walsh. He told the priest that he had never belonged to any religion but that he had always believed in God. He knew he had only a short time to live and wished to die in the Catholic faith. Through these last hours, Buffalo Bill was lucid much of the time, giving directions for his funeral to his family and friends. They included instructions for his burial, which was to take place four months later, on Decoration Day.[12]

On January 10, one day after he was baptized, William F. "Buffalo Bill" Cody died. The exact cause is not known; it could have been complications from a severe cold he contracted late that fall. Buffalo Bill drank little alcohol during the decade before his death, so that had no impact. His doctors did say that his heart had been seriously damaged by years of smoking. The cause of death was listed on the Certificate of Death as "ure-mic poisoning," a generic statement often used when the true reason for death was not clear. Under "occupation" the certificate bore one simple word: show-man. Buffalo Bill was many things, but that single word summed up the work that had occupied most of his life and for which he would be remembered.[13]

Upon notice of Buffalo Bill's death, telegrams of sympathy began to pour into Denver. They came from old friends like General Nelson Miles and John Burke. President Woodrow Wilson sent his sympathies as well. One of the more poignant telegrams was from Chief Jack Red Cloud of the Oglala Lakota. The Oglala had assembled in council at Pine Ridge and penned a message that included the statement that "the Oglalas

had found in Buffalo Bill a warm and lasting friend." It concluded that their sorrow in his passing was lightened "only in the belief of our meeting before the presence of our Wakan Tanka in the great hunting ground."[14]

Buffalo Bill, the showman, had two more shows to attend, his own funeral and burial. On January 14, about twenty-five thousand people passed by his coffin where it lay in the rotunda of the Colorado State Capitol. Thousands more watched the funeral procession as a caisson bore the casket to the Denver Elks Lodge Number 17. After the funeral, his body was taken to Olingers Mortuary, where it would be kept until Decoration Day.[15]

Surrounded by flowers, Buffalo Bill's casket lies in the Denver Elks Lodge during the funeral service.

Buffalo Bill first became a member of the Omaha, Nebraska, Elks Lodge in 1897. Less than a year after his 1916 membership certificate for the Omaha lodge was issued, the Denver Elks conducted his funeral ceremony in Denver. His casket was borne on a caisson through the streets of Denver from the Capitol to the Elks Lodge.

Eulogy

Delivered By

Col. John W. Springer, of Denver

At the Bier of

Colonel William Frederick Cody

"Buffalo Bill"

In the Home of Denver Lodge, No. 17, B. P. O. Elks

Sunday, January 14, 1917

COPYRIGHTED, 1917, BY HALSEY M. RHOADS, DENVER, COLORADO.

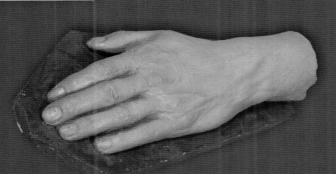

This cast of Buffalo Bill's left hand was made shortly before his death. It was later painted to look more realistic by Johnny Baker.

143

This burial permit for William F. Cody was issued on January 12, 1917, and noted that Olingers Mortuary would be the place where he initially resided. Later, after the specific site on Lookout Mountain was chosen by his family, the word *Olingers* was scratched out and *Lookout Mtn.* written in.

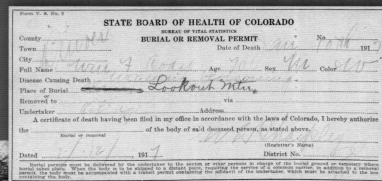

Visitors wait to view Cody's body before his burial on Lookout Mountain on June 3, 1917.

Quince Record poses at Buffalo Bill's grave after playing "Taps" during the burial.

The bugle played by Quince Record during Buffalo Bill's burial on Lookout Mountain was later decorated with gold braid.

144

When the family announced Buffalo Bill's wishes for his funeral, there was a surprise for the folks back in Cody, Wyoming. Buffalo Bill was not to be buried in their town but would be buried on Lookout Mountain, near Denver. Not one to dwell on issues like his final resting place, Cody had mentioned various sites over the years. At one point, he had talked about being buried with his children in Rochester. But on his deathbed, he had made a final decision.

All of the immediate members of Buffalo Bill's family were firm in their insistence that he had asked to be buried on Lookout Mountain. Louisa later wrote that they had expected he would ask to be buried near Cody but that he changed his mind. He told her, "I want to be buried on top of Mount Lookout. It's right over Denver. You can look down on four states there. It's pretty up there. I want to be buried up there—instead of in Wyoming." That he had asked to be buried on Lookout Mountain was affirmed by others as well, including the priest who had baptized him the day before his death.[16]

Upset by the announcement of Buffalo Bill's imminent burial on Lookout Mountain, some people in Cody produced an early will. On February 14, 1906, a year after his divorce from Louisa was denied, Will had drawn up a lengthy will dictating the disposition of his assets upon his death. This included bequests to his remaining daughter,

Irma; his foster son, Johnny Baker; and his grandchildren, nephews, sisters, and friends. Mention of his wife, Louisa, was conspicuously absent. He also asked that he be buried on Cedar Mountain, near Cody, Wyoming. In response to this revelation from Wyoming, the Cody family produced a later will, executed in North Platte, Nebraska, on February 19, 1913. In that will, which revoked all former wills, Buffalo Bill left his estate to his wife and designated her as his executrix. By that time, the two had been reconciled for nearly three years, which made the new will quite logical. Any hopes that people in Cody might have had for overthrowing the 1913 will were dashed on May 28, 1917, when the will was proven in the district court of Park County, Wyoming. Buffalo Bill had changed his mind, and there was little to be done about it.[17]

By June 3, 1917, everything was prepared for Buffalo Bill's burial on Lookout Mountain. The newly formed William F. Cody Memorial Association and members of the family had made several visits to determine the location of the grave. It was reported that daughter Irma had found two spots that she liked but decided to defer to the association and other family members. Finally, on May 17, Buffalo Bill's sister May Decker picked a rocky point in Denver's Lookout Mountain Park for the burial. Nearly everything had gone according to Buffalo Bill's request. The only change was that the burial date, originally slated for Decoration Day on May 30, was pushed back four days at the request of the Grand Army of the Republic. The GAR was concerned that its members would be participating in parades and unable to attend the burial on Decoration Day.[18]

The crowd that attended the burial, conducted by the Golden City Masonic Lodge on June 3, was almost as large as that which had filed by Buffalo Bill while he lay in the Colorado State Capitol building. It included family members, close friends, members of the GAR and other veterans groups, former *Wild West* cast members, and throngs of fans. Newspapers reported attendance at twenty thousand. Louisa Cody had ordered an open casket so that everyone could take one last look at Buffalo Bill before he was lowered into the ground. Buffalo Bill was gone but not forgotten. Over the following decades, his life would continue to inspire admiration and imitation, and his burial would continue to provoke controversy.[19]

Nearly six months after his death, Buffalo Bill was transported up Lookout Mountain to his final resting place. A Boy Scout and Denver police proudly guard his casket, opened for one final viewing.

Chapter Nine
The Legacy

I cannot express my feelings to you in words for you are so near and dear to my heart. For twenty-three years you have never once failed me. No Father ever had a son more loving and faithful. You have done as much to make Buffalo Bills *Wild West* what it is as I have myself. *Buffalo Bill, Letter to Johnny Baker, 1905*

Johnny Baker was stunned by Mary Jester Allen's actions. For some reason, Cody's niece was trying to undermine his every effort to memorialize Buffalo Bill. In all the years he had been by Cody's side, she had had little to do with her uncle or with the *Wild West*. But now that Louisa and daughter Irma had passed on, Mrs. Allen had mounted a campaign to move Buffalo Bill from his resting place on Lookout Mountain. That was not what the family had wanted; they had chosen the gravesite in keeping with Buffalo Bill's dying request. But Cody's niece had been agitating to remove Buffalo Bill ever since Johnny built his museum by the grave. Now she had written a letter to other family members criticizing his management of Buffalo Bill's gravesite.[1]

Two different drawings were submitted for the Pantheon of the Pioneers of America that was to be erected at Buffalo Bill's grave. One, featuring a giant statue of Buffalo Bill, was based upon a painting by Pappacena of Buffalo Bill scouting. Neither was built, due to inadequate funds.

Buffalo Bill was buried on Lookout Mountain in 1917 with very little controversy. Most folks appeared to agree with Memorial Association vice president Theodore Roosevelt's comment, "It seems to me peculiarly appropriate to erect the monument on a lofty perch like Lookout Mountain, the neighborhood of which to the city of Denver renders it easy at access for all our people—for Buffalo Bill was an American of all Americans."[2]

But not everyone agreed. In 1925, Buffalo Bill's niece Mary Jester Allen and a group of other relatives announced their intentions to move the body to Cody, Wyoming, beginning a controversy that has continued until today. The announcement by Mrs. Allen was immediately repudiated by Cody's two remaining sisters, Julia and May. May said, "I am not at all in favor of moving my brother. And I don't believe it can be done. The propaganda is just some crazy stunt—probably publicity. My brother loved Colorado—it wouldn't be fair to him." Johnny Baker was even more forthright: "I think the whole thing was started by the talk of people who had nothing else to talk about."[3]

These negative reactions from the three persons still alive who were closest to Buffalo Bill did nothing to dissuade Mary Jester Allen and her allies from their cause. She began writing letters to friends and family criticizing the conditions on Lookout Mountain and Johnny Baker himself. Before long, rumors surfaced that Louisa Cody had been given a bribe to have Buffalo Bill buried on Lookout Mountain. The rumors continued even after Johnny Baker issued a statement that insurance had paid for Buffalo Bill's funeral and no bribe had been offered or taken.[4]

Buffalo Bill was buried on Lookout Mountain just months after the United States entered World War I. Earlier, the William F. Cody Memorial Association had announced plans to create a massive monument, a Pantheon of the Pioneers of America, on Lookout Mountain. Two designs for the monument were submitted, each costing more than $1 million and housing a library, an art gallery, and a museum of frontier artifacts. Cody's grave would be in the rotunda of this tribute to the pioneers. In anticipation of this monument, the gravesite was initially simple, marked by a pile of stones, a wooden marker, and a flagpole. The Boy Scouts of America and schoolchildren everywhere began to raise money to contribute to the monument. Even George M. Cohan staged a special fund-raiser at the Broadway Theater in Denver. But, in February of 1918, Louisa Cody made an announcement that, in consideration of the war going on in Europe, plans for the monument would be postponed. "I know that my husband, were he to have his say, would place the needs of our country and its soldiers ahead of a memorial-building project."[5]

After Buffalo Bill's death in 1917, Johnny Baker and members of Cody's family organized a new show to carry on his legacy. But the nation's attention was focused on other things, and it closed after one season. Buffalo Bill's show would go on at the memorial on Lookout Mountain.

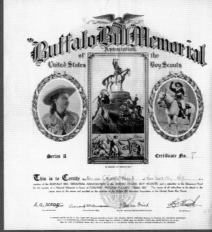

Johnny Baker had spent most of his life on the road with Buffalo Bill, living out of trunks like this. After Cody died in late 1917, forty-eight-year-old Baker had to find a new way of life.

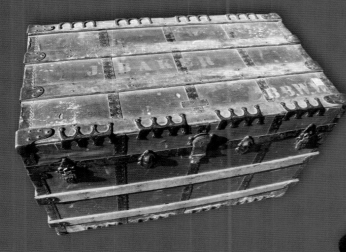

In 1917, a donation bin was placed by Buffalo Bill's gravesite to collect funds for the Pantheon of the Pioneers of America. It was provided by Denver businessmen Paul Weiss and Harry Tammen. Ironically, it was Tammen who had been responsible for the demise of *Buffalo Bill's Wild West* four years earlier.

On October 26, 1918, the *Rocky Mountain News* announced that Denver had placed a bronze plaque over Buffalo Bill's grave "to remain until after the war and the Cody memorial is erected." It was around that date that the first stone monument was erected and a fence placed around the grave. The enclosure also contained a lone pine tree. Despite several efforts to raise funds after the conclusion of World War I, the Pantheon of the Pioneers of America was never built. Then, on October 20, 1921, Louisa Cody died and was buried with her husband.[6]

After 1925, Mrs. Allen continued her efforts to have Buffalo Bill moved to Cody, Wyoming. Finally, in 1927, *The Denver Post* reported that Johnny Baker had reburied the Codys under twelve feet of reinforced concrete. According to Baker, "This work forever settles the idle talk about the possible removal of the bodies of Colonel Cody and Mrs. Cody from the resting place they chose." Baker contended that "our work has been done to make perpetual the lasting resting place of Colonel and Mrs. Cody and to provide a sure foundation for any monument that may be erected in the future."[7]

Unfortunately, the burial of Buffalo Bill and Louisa under twelve feet of concrete did not settle the idle talk. In 1948, the Colorado National Guard stationed troops around the grave when the Cody American Legion Post offered a $10,000 reward to anyone who would steal Buffalo Bill's body. Threats to remove the body continued throughout the twentieth century. Eventually the controversy created its own lore. A 1919 photograph of a tank at the grave was interpreted as protecting Buffalo Bill from Wyoming grave robbers. It actually was there for a war bond drive and fired a salute over the grave. A few years later, a group of cowboys started for Denver with the intent of reclaiming Buffalo Bill's body for Wyoming. According to the story, they got as far as a bar in Casper, where they drank too much and forgot their mission. After years of these failures, real or imagined, to rob Cody's grave, a new rumor emerged in the 1990s. It alleged that Buffalo Bill's corpse was replaced with that of a derelict while it lay in Olingers Mortuary. Buffalo Bill himself was spirited away to an unmarked grave in Cody before the burial. As with most rumors, there is

For several months, Buffalo Bill's grave was marked by a simple pile of stones, a flagpole, and a wooden sign on a lone tree. In 1918, it was surrounded by a fence, and a monument of quartz was placed on the grave.

One October in the late 1920s, a caretaker at Pahaska Tepee spread a rumor that some people from Cody, Wyoming, were trying to steal Buffalo Bill's body. Johnny Baker, who was in Denver at the time, bought this .38-caliber Smith and Wesson and returned to the gravesite, aiming "to shoot the hell out of them." The body was safe, the caretaker got in trouble, and the gun entered the museum's collection after Johnny's death in 1931.

For many years, it was believed this tank was posted at the grave to protect Buffalo Bill's body from Wyoming grave robbers. Recent research has shown it was at the grave in 1919 to promote a war bond drive. The controversy over Buffalo Bill's burial on Lookout Mountain did not begin until the 1920s.

the feet of Buffalo Bill. He intended to continue in show business but to also ensure his foster father got the recognition he deserved. After Buffalo Bill's Denver funeral, Baker joined with Cody's widow, Louisa, and daughter Irma in incorporating the *Buffalo Bill Wild West Exhibition*. Like the original *Wild West*, it would have American Indians, cowboys, sharpshooters, and riders demonstrating horsemanship. Including a collection of paintings and other artifacts from Buffalo Bill's life, the new exhibition hit the road in 1917 with the slogan "Let My Show Go On." But the show did not go on. The United States entered World War I in April, and the public's attention was focused elsewhere. Following a disappointing season, the show folded. Johnny had to find something else to do.[9]

The Pantheon of Pioneers of America was never built, but in its absence Johnny Baker created a more modest and perhaps more fitting memorialization of his foster father for the thousands of people who visited Buffalo Bill's gravesite each year. In 1920, he wrote a letter to the City of Denver with a proposal:

no documentation or logic to support the story. In fact, any imposter would have been discovered when Louisa ordered the casket opened at the burial ceremony on Lookout Mountain. Despite Johnny Baker's best efforts, however, the disagreement over Buffalo Bill's final resting place continues.[8]

The loss of Buffalo Bill in 1917 left a big gap in Johnny Baker's life. His whole life had been show business, learned at

I have a collection which would be of great interest to the visitors to Lookout Mountain, and if it is possible to get a location adjacent to his tomb, I would erect a building to conform to the architecture of the Mountain Parks scheme.[10]

151

Baker's Pahaska Tepee, named after Buffalo Bill's hunting lodge near Yellowstone, opened on Memorial Day of 1921. It was filled with artifacts from Buffalo Bill that belonged to Johnny Baker, Louisa Cody, and friends of the family. These included the famous rifle Lucretia Borgia, Yellow Hair's scalp, Rosa Bonheur's painting, and a variety of personal items from Buffalo Bill. Admission to the Buffalo Bill Memorial Museum portion of the building was free, so Baker operated a restaurant and gift shop to provide funds for the facility's operation.

When Louisa Cody died a few months later, her artifacts in the museum became part of her estate. Lucretia Borgia, Yellow Hair's scalp and the knife Buffalo Bill used to take it, Sitting Bull's scalp shirt, all originally part of the Buffalo Bill Memorial Museum, were returned to Will and Louisa's descendants. The Bonheur painting of Buffalo Bill as well as other paintings that Buffalo Bill had commissioned from artist friends were to be sold. A painting of Buffalo Bill by the Italian painter Pappacena had already been presented to the City of Denver by Louisa, so it stayed as a centerpiece of the museum. Of all of his paintings, according to Louisa, this was Buffalo Bill's favorite.[11]

Meanwhile, back in Wyoming, Mary Jester Allen had begun to collect artifacts for a museum. When she and some Cody family members met in 1925 and issued their call for Buffalo Bill's body to be moved to Wyoming, they had also formed the Cody Family Association. During the meeting they named Allen chair of an effort to create a museum in the town of Cody. That museum was opened on July 4, 1927, in a structure built to resemble the main house at Buffalo Bill's TE Ranch. America now had two Buffalo Bill Memorial Museums, one in Cody, Wyoming, and the other on Lookout Mountain near Denver.[12]

Over the next several years, some of the artifacts from Louisa's estate stayed at Baker's museum while others were removed by the family. Some were given to Allen's new museum while others were sold. Through time, each Buffalo Bill Memorial Museum amassed separate collections, each collection commemorating the life of the great scout and showman. While Mary Jester Allen and Johnny Baker never buried the hatchet, they each concentrated more on their

In 1920, Johnny Baker petitioned the City of Denver to erect a museum and gift shop down the hill from Buffalo Bill's grave. Pahaska Tepee was opened on Memorial Day, 1921.

This is the earliest photo of Johnny Baker's museum, taken around 1922 (left). Buffalo Bill's rifle Lucretia Borgia and Yellow Hair's scalp are on exhibit on one wall. They were later returned to Buffalo Bill's descendants.

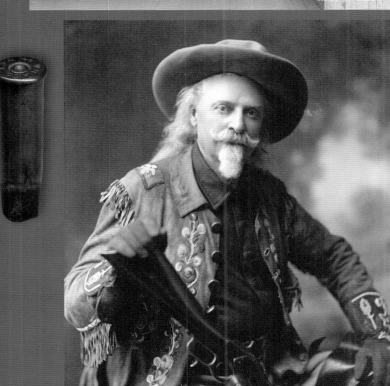

When Johnny Baker proposed to build a museum near Buffalo Bill's grave, he wrote the City of Denver that he had many of Buffalo Bill's personal effects, such as guns, saddles, and show outfits as well as this, the cartridge from Buffalo Bill's last shot.

Visitors to Johnny Baker's Pahaska Tepee (above) could visit the Buffalo Bill Memorial Museum, purchase gifts and a meal, and enjoy a spectacular view of Denver.

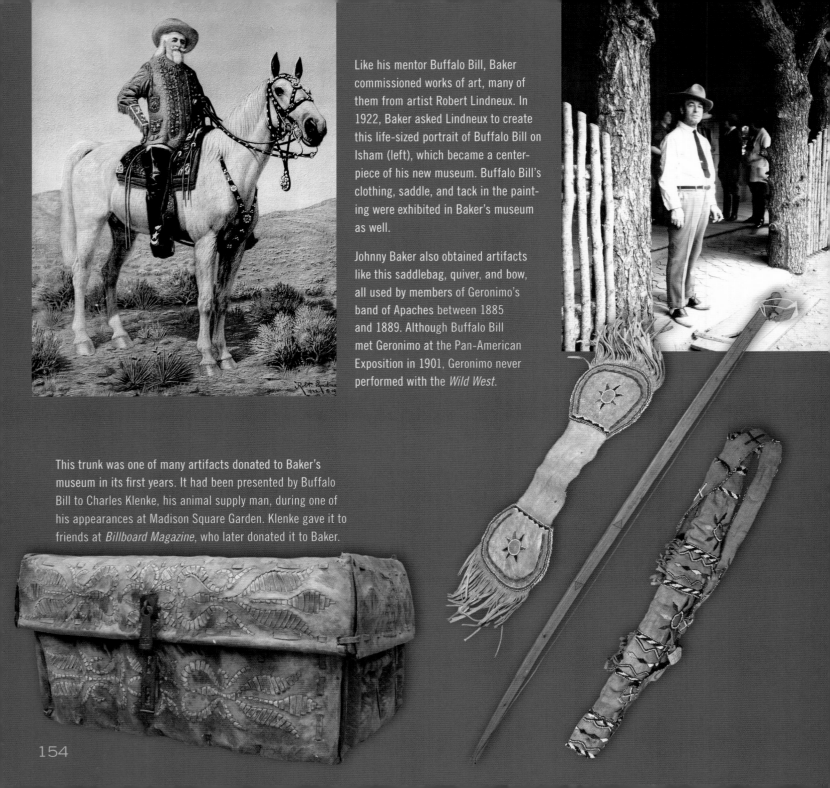

Like his mentor Buffalo Bill, Baker commissioned works of art, many of them from artist Robert Lindneux. In 1922, Baker asked Lindneux to create this life-sized portrait of Buffalo Bill on Isham (left), which became a centerpiece of his new museum. Buffalo Bill's clothing, saddle, and tack in the painting were exhibited in Baker's museum as well.

Johnny Baker also obtained artifacts like this saddlebag, quiver, and bow, all used by members of Geronimo's band of Apaches between 1885 and 1889. Although Buffalo Bill met Geronimo at the Pan-American Exposition in 1901, Geronimo never performed with the *Wild West*.

This trunk was one of many artifacts donated to Baker's museum in its first years. It had been presented by Buffalo Bill to Charles Klenke, his animal supply man, during one of his appearances at Madison Square Garden. Klenke gave it to friends at *Billboard Magazine*, who later donated it to Baker.

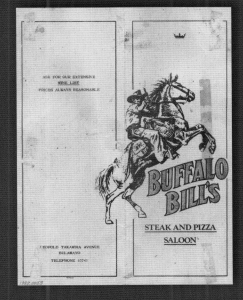

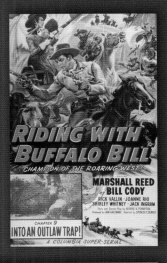

In addition to making early Westerns and laying the groundwork for the Western movie genre, Buffalo Bill has been featured in more than forty movies, plays, and television programs since his death.

Buffalo Bill's popularity has spread throughout the world in the nearly one hundred years since his death. Today his name is seen on everything from a saloon in Zimbabwe to comic books in Europe (left). Visitors to Disneyland Paris enjoy two showings of a revived *Wild West* every evening.

respective museums and less on each other. Eventually, new buildings were erected, new stories were told, and new names were created. Today, the Buffalo Bill Museum and Grave on Lookout Mountain and the Buffalo Bill Historical Center in Cody, Wyoming, are each a critical part of William F. Cody's legacy.

As Teddy Roosevelt observed, Buffalo Bill was an "American of all Americans" whose story belonged to the country. Eventually his Scout's Rest Ranch outside North Platte became a historic house museum maintained by the State of Nebraska. A Buffalo Bill Museum was opened in his birthplace of Le Claire, Iowa. Today, Buffalo Bill's legacy is preserved and interpreted in museums throughout the United States as well as in Europe.

Buffalo Bill's legacy has a long reach. His innovations in show operations were studied and copied by many during his time. The "cowboy's fun" portion of his *Wild West*, with its races and bucking bronco riding, has been credited with helping originate professional rodeo. The popularity of *Buffalo Bill's Wild West* and its imitators influenced the fledgling movie industry to focus on western themes, making Western movies one of the earliest film genres.

Some of Buffalo Bill's other influences on popular culture are less obvious but no less important. His promotion of "The Star-Spangled Banner" in his shows helped influence the song's choice as the American national anthem. His brief and somewhat catastrophic stay in New Orleans during 1885 even had its influence on American popular music. Inspired by *Buffalo Bill's Wild West*, African Americans in New Orleans began dressing as American Indians during Mardi Gras. The Mardi Gras Indian tribes imitated the clothing and language of the Plains Indians, singing songs like "Iko, Iko" while they marched. Those songs in turn influenced jazz, rhythm and blues, and rock and roll.

In 1923, Johnny Baker hosted Lakota chief Spotted Weasel and a group of braves who came to pay tribute to Buffalo Bill. After posing at Pahaska Tepee, they placed Indian head nickels on the grave.

A tireless booster of the West, Buffalo Bill promoted it as a destination for tourists and settlers. William Cody carried on his father Isaac's work, founding the town of Cody, a thriving community at the eastern gateway to Yellowstone National Park, a place he helped promote. An advocate for development of the West, he also championed equal rights for American Indians and spoke of the need to preserve wilderness.

After his death, one of Denver's newspapers eulogized William F. Cody as being "the spirit of the West, typical of the West, one of her favored and her favorite sons." Buffalo Bill's body may be buried on Lookout Mountain, but his spirit is still alive. His name is recognized throughout the world, and he is one of America's best-known historical figures. Today, William F. "Buffalo Bill" Cody, child of the West, has become both a legend and symbol of the West and of America.

Painted in 1892 by Pappacena, an Italian artist, this painting was Cody's favorite portrait of himself. Depicting Buffalo Bill as a scout, the painting was later used for several *Wild West* posters. It was presented to the City of Denver by Louisa Cody and became a centerpiece of the Buffalo Bill Memorial Museum.

Notes

Chapter One: A Life in the Outdoors, 1846–1866

1. William F. Cody, *The Life of Hon. William F. Cody Known as Buffalo Bill the Famous Hunter, Scout and Guide* (1879; repr., Lincoln: Univ. of Nebraska Press, 1978), 48, 91.
2. Ibid., 26; Don Russell, "Julia Cody Goodman's Memoirs of Buffalo Bill," *Kansas Historical Quarterly* 28, no. 4 (Winter 1962): 455.
3. Cody, *The Life of Hon. William F. Cody*, 40–42, 43, 45–46, 48.
4. Ibid., 57–58, 73.
5. Ibid., 72.
6. Ibid., 103.
7. Alexander Majors, *Seventy Years on the Frontier* (1893; repr., Minneapolis: Ross and Haines, 1965), 176–177.
8. Cody, *The Life of Hon. William F. Cody*, 127.
9. Ibid., 134; Frank Winch, "Chronological History of William Frederick Cody 'Buffalo Bill'" unpublished manuscript, n.d., Buffalo Bill Museum and Grave Archives, Golden, CO, 78.
10. Cody, *The Life of Hon. William F. Cody*, 135; Don Russell, *The Lives and Legends of Buffalo Bill* (Norman: Univ. of Oklahoma Press, 1960), 72.

Chapter Two: Will Cody Becomes Buffalo Bill, 1867–1872

1. Cody, *The Life of Hon. William F. Cody*, 155.
2. Ibid., 174; Russell, *The Lives and Legends*, 92–94.
3. Cody, *The Life of Hon. William F. Cody*, 162; Russell, *The Lives and Legends*, 346.
4. Russell, *The Lives and Legends*, 160.
5. Ibid., 133, 138, 147.
6. Department of the Army Board for Correction of Military Records, "Supplemental Proceedings in the Case of Cody, William F. (Deceased)," Docket AC88-10374, May 3, 1989.
7. Russell, *The Lives and Legends*, 155, 159.
8. Cody, *The Life of Hon. William F. Cody*, 266–267, 279–280.
9. Ibid., 301.
10. Ibid., 308; Nellie Snyder Yost, *Buffalo Bill, His Family, Friends, Fame, Failures, and Fortunes* (Athens, OH: Swallow Press, 1979), 72, 99.
11. Cody, *The Life of Hon. William F. Cody*, 309.
12. Ibid., 311.

Chapter Three: Buffalo Bill's New Career, 1873–1878

1. Cody, *The Life of Hon. William F. Cody*, 321; Sandra K. Sagala, *Buffalo Bill on Stage* (Albuquerque: Univ. of New Mexico Press, 2008), 19.
2. Cody, *The Life of Hon. William F. Cody*, 323–324.
3. Sagala, *Buffalo Bill on Stage*, 33.
4. Louis S. Warren, *Buffalo Bill's America: William Cody and the Wild West Show* (New York: Alfred A. Knopf, 2005), 157.
5. Cody, *The Life of Hon. William F. Cody*, 328.
6. Ibid., 332–333.

7. Russell, *The Lives and Legends*, 266–269.
8. Cody, *The Life of Hon. William F. Cody*, 339.
9. Russell, *The Lives and Legends*, 219, 222.
10. Christian Madsen Papers, 1929–1934, Buffalo Bill Museum and Grave Archives, Golden, CO; "Relics of Buffalo Bill," *Baltimore Sun*, in Buffalo Bill's 1907 Season Scrapbook, Buffalo Bill Historical Center Collection, Cody, WY.
11. Captain Charles King, *Campaigning with Crook and Stories of Army Life* (1890; repr., Ann Arbor: Univ. of Michigan Microfilms, 1966), 42.
12. Christian Madsen Papers, 1929–1934, Buffalo Bill Museum and Grave Archives, Golden, CO.
13. Cody, *The Life of Hon. William F. Cody*, 336.
14. Ibid., 360–361.

Chapter Four: Seeking Authenticity, 1879–1886

1. William F. Cody, *Story of the Wild West and Campfire Chats* (Richmond, VA: B. F. Johnson and Company, 1888), 691–692.
2. Sagala, *Buffalo Bill on Stage*, 101–105.
3. Russell, *The Lives and Legends*, 263; "Home and Society," *Colorado Transcript*, July 23, 1879, 3.
4. Cody, *Story of the Wild West*, 693–694.
5. Yost, *Buffalo Bill*, 116–122; Frank Winch, *Thrilling Lives of Buffalo Bill and Pawnee Bill* (New York:

S. L. Parsons and Co., 1911), 175–177.

6. Home Matters, *Fort Collins (CO) Courier*, May 24, 1883, 4; April 19, 1883, 3; and March 29, 1883, 4; Russell, *The Lives and Legends*, 295–296.

7. Yost, *Buffalo Bill*, 128; Russell, *The Lives and Legends*, 296; Richard J. Walsh, *The Making of Buffalo Bill* (Chicago: A. L. Burt Company, 1928), 212–214.

8. "Col. Cody Is Reminiscent," *Duluth (MN) Herald*, May 20, 1910.

9. Winch, "Chronological History," 80.

10. Yost, *Buffalo Bill*, 131; Russell, *The Lives and Legends*, 295; "The Wild West," *Bloomington Bulletin*, May 24, 1883, 3.

11. Cody, *Story of the Wild West*, 694.

12. Mark Twain to Bill Cody, Sept. 10, 1884, Mark Twain Papers, Bancroft Library, Univ. of California at Berkeley.

13. Cody, *Story of the Wild West*, 699.

14. Russell, *The Lives and Legends*, 309.

15. Walsh, *The Making of Buffalo Bill*, 242–243; Cody, *Story of the Wild West*, 699.

16. Russell, *The Lives and Legends*, 311, 313.

17. Robert M. Utley, *The Lance and the Shield: The Life and Times of Sitting Bull* (New York: Ballantine Books, 1993), 263–264; L. G. Moses, *Wild West Shows and Images of American Indians: 1883–1933* (Albuquerque: Univ. of New Mexico Press, 1996), 28.

18. Bobby Bridger, *Buffalo Bill and Sitting Bull: Inventing the Wild West* (Austin: Univ. of Texas Press, 2002), 320; Sitting Bull to President Grover Cleveland, June 23, 1885, #14386-

1885 of Record Group 75, National Archives and Records Administration, Washington DC; "Tracking the 'Messiah,'" *New York Tribune Weekly*, November 26, 1890; W. Fletcher Johnson, *Life of Sitting Bull and History of the Indian War of 1890–91* (Philadelphia: Edgewood Publishing, 1891), 193; William F. Cody, *True Tales of the Plains* (New York: Cupples and Leon Company, 1908), 247.

19. Sagala, *Buffalo Bill on Stage*, 189.

20. Walsh, *The Making of Buffalo Bill*, 262; Cody, *Story of the Wild West*, 700.

21. Stella Foote, *Letters from Buffalo Bill* (El Segundo, CA: Upton and Sons, 1950), 33.

22. Cody, *Story of the Wild West*, 700; Foote, *Letters from Buffalo Bill*, 26; Mark Twain to Bill Cody, Sept. 10, 1884, Bancroft Library, Univer. of California at Berkeley.

Chapter Five: Americans and Europeans, 1887–1892

1. "Buffalo Bill Visits NCR Plant and Addresses the Officers Club," n.p., n.d., in Buffalo Bill's 1907 Season Scrapbook, Buffalo Bill Historical Center Collection, Cody, WY; "Statue of Indian for City's Harbor," n.p., n.d., in Buffalo Bill's 1909–1910 Season Scrapbook, Buffalo Bill Historical Center Collection, Cody, WY.

2. Cody, *Story of the Wild West*, 704–706.

3. William F. Cody's Private Scrapbook, 1887–1890, Buffalo Bill Museum and Grave Collection, Golden, CO; "London Society" notice, reprinted in *Brooklyn Daily Eagle*, July 31, 1887; Cody, *Story of the Wild West*, 724–725, 749.

4. Cody, *Story of the Wild West*, 735–737.

5. Ibid., 757.

6. Yost, *Buffalo Bill*, 213–216.

7. "At the Great Exhibition Opened," *Brooklyn Daily Eagle*, May 3, 1889.

8. "A Visit to Paris," *Brooklyn Daily Eagle*, September 13, 1889; Moses, *Wild West Shows and Images*, 82; Dahesh Museum, *Rosa Bonheur: All Nature's Children* (New York: Dahesh Museum, 1998), 20–21.

9. Joseph Harris, *The Tallest Tower: Eiffel & the Belle Epoque* (Washington, DC: Regnery Gateway, 1975), 118; Moses, *Wild West Shows and Images*, 82–83.

10. Russell, *The Lives and Legends*, 352; Yost, *Buffalo Bill*, 224.

11. John M. Burke, *"Buffalo Bill" from Prairie to Palace* (New York: Rand, McNally and Company, 1893), 239.

12. Moses, *Wild West Shows and Images*, 103–104; Russell, *The Lives and Legends*, 352.

13. Sam Maddra, *Hostiles? The Lakota Ghost Dance and Buffalo Bill's Wild West* (Norman: Univ. of Oklahoma Press, 2006), 28–29, 42–44.

14. George Crager, "As Narrated by 'Short Bull,'" unpublished manuscript based upon an oral account by Short Bull, ca. 1891, Buffalo Bill Museum and Grave Archives, Golden, CO; Maddra, *Hostiles*, 21.

15. Crager, "As Narrated by 'Short Bull.'"

16. Dispatch from General Nelson Miles to Colonel William F. Cody, November 24, 1890, Buffalo Bill Museum and Grave Archives, Golden, CO; Bridger, *Buffalo Bill and Sitting Bull*, 380–381.

17. General Nelson Miles to Colonel

William F. Cody, December 4, 1890, Buffalo Bill Museum and Grave Archives, Golden, CO; Utley, *The Lance*, 298–302.

18. Crager, "As Narrated by 'Short Bull'"; Maddra, *Hostiles*, 61.

19. Governor Thayer to William F. Cody, January 6, 1891, Buffalo Bill Museum and Grave Archives, Golden, CO; Crager, "As Narrated by 'Short Bull'"; Russell, *The Lives and Legends*, 368.

20. Russell, *The Lives and Legends*, 370.

21. Crager, "As Narrated by 'Short Bull.'"

Chapter Six: Rough Riding to Riches, 1893–1904

1. Buffalo Bill's 1892 Season Scrapbook, Buffalo Bill Museum and Grave Archives, Golden, CO.

2. Walsh, *The Making of Buffalo Bill*, 299–300.

3. Robert A. Carter, *Buffalo Bill Cody: The Man Behind the Legend* (New York: John Wiley and Sons, Inc., 2000), 372.

4. Erik Larson, *The Devil in the White City* (New York: Vintage Books Edition, 2004), 286; "Colonel Cody on the Sex Problem," *Buffalo Bill's Wild West and Congress of Rough Riders of the World* 1899 program, 27, Buffalo Bill Museum and Grave Archives, Golden, CO; Alice J. McChesney to her Uncle John, September 25, 1916, Buffalo Bill Museum and Grave Archives, Golden, CO.

5. Irakli Makharadze and Akaki Chkhaidze, *Wild West Georgians* (Tblisi, Republic of Georgia: New Media Tblisi, 2001), 5–8.

6. Russell, *The Lives and Legends*, 375; "The Magic City: A Portfolio of Original Photographic Views of the Great World's Fair," *Historical Fine Arts Series*, April 23, 1894, Buffalo Bill Museum and Grave Archives, Golden, CO.

7. Yost, *Buffalo Bill*, 245, 247–251.

8. Russell, *The Lives and Legends*, 422–423.

9. Ibid., 424.

10. Frank Winch, "How Buffalo Bill Is to Spend His Time," publicity brochure, ca. 1911, Buffalo Bill Historical Center Collection, Cody, WY.

11. Richard Bonner, *William F. Cody's Wyoming Empire* (Norman: Univ. of Oklahoma Press, 2007), 7.

12. Jeannie Cook, Lynne Johnson Houze, Bob Edgar, and Paul Fees, *Buffalo Bill's Town in the Rockies* (Virginia Beach, VA: Donning Company Publishers, 1996), 48.

13. "Wild Western Sports," *Brooklyn Daily Eagle*, May 13, 1894.

14. Russell, *The Lives and Legends*, 378–379.

15. Ibid., 420.

16. Sarah J. Blackstone, *Buckskin, Bullets, and Business: A History of Buffalo Bill's Wild West* (New York: Greenwood Press, 1986), 28.

17. Foote, *Letters from Buffalo Bill*, 90; "Cody Seeks a Divorce," *Colorado Transcript*, March 17, 1904.

Chapter Seven: Friends, Family, and Faith, 1905–1912

1. Foote, *Letters from Buffalo Bill*, 87; Walsh, *The Making of Buffalo Bill*, 243; Will Cody to Julia Cody Goodman, June 14, 1905. Buffalo Bill Historical Center Collection, Cody, WY.

2. Steve Friesen, "No Swearing or Drinking in My Company Since I Got Good," *Points West* (Winter 2003): 21–22.

3. Yost, *Buffalo Bill*, 322–335; "Buffalo Bill's Divorce Suit Dismissed," *London Telegraph*, March 25, 1905, n.p. and n.d.; Clipping in 1905 Season Scrapbook, Buffalo Bill Historical Center Collection, Cody, WY.

4. "Cody and His Wife Make Up" and "Cody and Wife United," March 26, 1910, n.p. and n.d. in Mrs. Pony Bob Haslam's Scrapbook, Buffalo Bill Museum and Grave Archives, Golden, CO; Yost, *Buffalo Bill*, 364.

5. Russell, *The Lives and Legends*, 446–447.

6. Will Cody to Johnny Baker , November 12, 1905. Buffalo Bill Museum and Grave Archives, Golden, CO.

7. Julie Parker, "Treatment of a Native American Headdress from *Buffalo Bill's Wild West Show*," *Scout's Dispatch* (Buffalo Bill Museum and Grave newsletter) (Spring 2007); W. Hudson Kensel, *Pahaska Tepee* (Cody, WY: Buffalo Bill Historical Center, 1987), 4; Sarah J. Blackstone, *The Business of Being Buffalo Bill* (New York: Praeger Publishers, 1988), 92.

8. Yost, *Buffalo Bill*, 337.

9. Russell, *The Lives and Legends*, 443.

10. Winch, *Thrilling Lives*, 223.

Chapter Eight: The Final Stands, 1913–1917

1. Walsh, *The Making of Buffalo Bill*, 342; Russell, *The Lives and Legends*, 453.

2. Russell, *The Lives and Legends*, 453–455.

3. Yost, *Buffalo Bill*, 384; "Half of *Wild West* Show Sold at Auction for High Prices," *The Denver Post*, August 27, 1913, 3.

4. "Buffalo Bill Must Sacrifice Famous Horse on Auction Block,"

The Denver Post, August 19, 1913, 1; "Colonel Cody's Friends Outbid Each Other to Give Isham Back," *The Denver Post*, August 21, 1913, 1, 4.

5. Foote, *Letters from Buffalo Bill*, 144.

6. Yost, *Buffalo Bill*, 388–390.

7. Russell, *The Lives and Legends*, 458–459.

8. Walsh, *The Making of Buffalo Bill*, 353–354.

9. Ibid., 352; Russell, *The Lives and Legends*, 461.

10. Russell, *The Lives and Legends*, 461–464.

11. Walsh, *The Making of Buffalo Bill*, 356; Michael Wallis, *The Real Wild West: The 101 Ranch and the Creation of the American West* (New York: St. Martin's Press, 1999), 436–438.

12. "Cody Became a Catholic on His Deathbed," *The Denver Post*, January 11, 1917; "Noted Scout Loses His Last Battle," January 10, 1917, newspaper clipping n.p. in Mrs. Pony Bob Haslam's Scrapbook, Buffalo Bill Museum and Grave Archives, Golden, CO.

13. "Col. Cody Dies; Mountain Top Resting Place," January 10, 1917, newspaper clipping in Buffalo Bill Museum and Grave Archives, Golden, CO; Certified copy of William F. Cody Certificate of Death, State of Colorado Bureau of Vital Statistics, Denver, CO.

14. Blackstone, *The Business of Being Buffalo Bill*, 81–84.

15. "25,000 Pass Cody's Bier," *The New York Times*, January 15, 1917.

16. Louisa Frederici Cody, *Memories of Buffalo Bill* (New York: D. Appleton and Co., 1919), 324; Christopher Walsh to J. F. Hynes, Miami, Florida, June 13, 1927, Department of

Archives and Manuscripts, The Catholic University of America, Washington, DC.

17. William F. Cody Last Will and Testament, February 14, 1906; William F. Cody Last Will and Testament, February 19, 1913; and Testimony Proving Will of William F. Cody, May 28, 1917, Buffalo Bill Historical Center Collection, Cody, WY.

18. "Local Paragraphs," *Colorado Transcript*, January 11, 1917, 8; March 8, 1917, 8; May 17, 1917, 8; "Famous Scout's Daughter Here," *Colorado Transcript*, April 5, 1917, 4; "Dates for Coming Events," *Haswell (CO) Herald*, March 15, 1917, 11.

19. "Young and Old Pay Honor to 'Buffalo Bill,'" *The Denver Post*, June 4, 1917.

Chapter Nine: The Legacy

1. Buffalo Bill to Johnny Baker, November 12, 1905, Buffalo Bill Museum and Grave Archives, Golden, CO; Mary Jester Allen to Rose Odell, ca. 1925, Buffalo Bill Museum and Grave Archives, Golden, CO.

2. Quoted in Louis E. Cooke, "A Final Chapter in the Life Story of Co. Wm. F. Cody Buffalo Bill," unpublished manuscript, ca. 1922, Buffalo Bill Museum and Grave Archives, Golden, CO.

3. "Relatives of 'Buffalo Bill' in Chicago Start Movement to Take Body from Lookout," *The Denver Post*, October 28, 1925, 16.

4. Signed Statement from Johnny Baker, September 30, 1928, Buffalo Bill Museum and Grave Archives, Golden, CO.

5. "Cohan and Harris to Give Big Matinee Here for Cody Fund," *The Denver Post*, January 28, 1917;

"Postpone Building of Memorial," *Colorado Transcript*, February 21, 1918.

6. "Denver Marks Grave of Scout," *Rocky Mountain News*, October 26, 1918; "Body of Mrs. Cody Buried with That of Her Husband," *The Denver Post*, November 1, 1921.

7. "Tomb for Buffalo Bill Built to Last Forever," *The Denver Post*, November 23, 1927.

8. "Thank You, We'll Keep Him," *Rocky Mountain News*, August 2, 1948; "Little Zeb Was on the Job," *Carbonate (Leadville, CO) Chronicle*, April 28, 1919; "Buffalo Bill: The Man with Two Graves?" *EnCompass* (July/August 2008), 16–17.

9. "*Buffalo Bill's Wild West Show* Organized, Perpetuate Memory," *Northern Wyoming Herald*, January 19, 1917; Russell, *The Lives and Legends*, 473–474.

10. Johnny Baker to Denver Mountain Parks Advisory Committee, January 28, 1920, Buffalo Bill Museum and Grave Archives, Golden, CO.

11. "Will of Widow of Buffalo Bill Is Filed for Probate," *Fort Collins (CO) Courier*, October 28, 1921; "National Memorial to 'Buffalo Bill' Will Stand on a Mountain Top with Outlook Over Four States," *Columbus (OH) Sunday Dispatch*, March 4, 1917.

12. Juti Winchester, "All the West's a Stage: Buffalo Bill, Cody, Wyoming and Western Stage Heritage Presentation, 1846–1997" (PhD diss., Northern Arizona University, 1999), 140–141.

Index